Business Organisation and Management

GEOFF HARDERN
Trent Polytechnic, Nottingham

Philip Allan

First published 1978 by

PHILIP ALLAN PUBLISHERS LIMITED
MARKET PLACE
DEDDINGTON
OXFORD OX5 4SE

Reprinted 1979, 1981, 1984

© Geoff Hardern 1978

0 86003 506 9 (hardback)
0 86003 606 5 (paperback)

Typeset in 11/12pt IBM Baskerville by
MHL Typesetting Ltd, Coventry
Printed and bound in Great Britain at
The Camelot Press Ltd, Southampton

Contents

Preface

One of the most significant trends in higher education in recent years has been the growth of student numbers on a range of courses in business and management studies. To a large extent the popularity of these courses has reflected the continuing demand for able men and women to take positions of responsibility in complex enterprises operating in an uncertain business environment. This vocational interest in management education has been matched by a steady growth of books and articles about business organisation, management functions and techniques, business policy and the business environment from both academics and practising managers. Although some of this work is within established academic disciplines, new business specialisms such as decision analysis, corporate planning and organisation development have emerged as separate fields of study. The purpose of much of this literature is to suggest ways of improving management efficiency; other writers are more concerned with the general aims and objectives of business. Business is an exciting and rapidly developing field of study.

Unfortunately, this wide variety of specialisms, approaches and perspectives often seems like the confusion of tongues at Babel to the student embarking on a business course. Although he will need to explore some of these specialisms in depth if he is to become an effective manager, the student also needs to have a clear overview of the subject. The study of business should be more than a collection of unrelated specialist studies.

This book is an attempt to provide such a general survey of a wide and complex subject: the organisation and management of the modern business enterprise. It is not a textbook of business policy; this subject is best approached after some study of the basic business disciplines. Nor is it intended as an encyclopaedia of everything a successful manager needs to know. Even if such an aim were desirable, nobody would imagine that it could be achieved in a book of less than 200 pages. The book will have achieved its object if it encourages the reader to follow up some of the suggestions for further reading on pages 172–6.

It will be clear from this preamble that the book is intended primarily for students who are starting their studies of business or management at either undergraduate, diploma or postgraduate level. Science and technology students requiring a general appreciation of business may also find the book useful. It could serve as a basic text for the core modules entitled 'The Organisation in its Environment' in the new BEC national award courses. The integrated, case approach adopted in the book is in line with the underlying educational philosophy of BEC as set out in its First Policy Statement.

An extended case study is incorporated in the text to illustrate the main activities of a modern manufacturing business. Although the case is not intended primarily as a problem solving exercise, readers may wish to consider some of the issues for discussion raised in Appendix 2 after reading the whole of the case study. No apology is made for the inclusion of a fair amount of detailed production, marketing and financial information about 'Small Print' in an introductory text. The case is complex because business is complex and it seems important for the student to appreciate the richness of business activity from the start. The Robinson Crusoe approach to the study of business can be misleading as well as unrealistic.

Although the Small Print case study attempts to bring an element of realism into the exposition, the company is, in fact, fictitious. Some of the technical and marketing information is based on material collected by my colleague, Dr David

Jennings, from a progressive company in the same industry as Small Print. Financial and personnel material is drawn from different sources. All this detail has been modified in the interests of confidentiality, ease of exposition and the need to write certain 'problems' into the case. We would like to thank all the managers who have assisted us in the preparation of case materials.

I am grateful to *The Guardian* for permission to quote from an article on changing technology in the newspaper industry (see p. 107). Butterworths have kindly allowed me to use a modified version of a diagram on budgetary control in F.P. Langley, *Introduction to Accounting for Business Studies,* the third edition of which is due to be published in 1978 (see p. 122).

I have been particularly fortunate in having the help and encouragement of my colleagues at Trent Polytechnic. In addition to his help with the case study, David Jennings has given me invaluable advice on the incorporation of this material into the text. The financial aspects of the case study are based on material originally prepared by Alan Lovell. Ray Lye, Cyril Wootton, Mike Bird, Ralph Bedrock and Peter Clarke have read through sections of the book and saved me from many errors. I have also benefitted immensely from discussion with these and other colleagues about matters of approach and emphasis. In particular, Dr W. Duncan Reekie made helpful suggestions about the structure of the book. I must, of course, bear full responsibility for all errors of commission, omission and emphasis.

I have been fortunate in having the expert help of Paula Leigh and Anne Ipgrave in the preparation of a difficult manuscript. My daughter Claire has kept me supplied with innumerable cups of coffee and put me right about the linear programming example. Finally, I should like to thank my wife, Sheila. She has been a constant source of support and encouragement during the writing of this book and has helped at all stages of its preparation.

Geoff Hardern
Nottingham, November 1977

CHAPTER 1
Introduction

This book is about business and the study of business. What then is the scope of our subject? Is it possible to define with any precision the wide range of activities, objectives and organisations which we commonly associate with the idea of business? The main difficulty is that 'business' is a chameleon-like word which takes on a different meaning as the context changes, as in President Coolidge's famous aphorism that 'the business of the United States is business'.

If we examine the images which come to mind when we think about 'business' or talk about a 'business enterprise', 'businessmen', or 'business skills', we should be able to identify two overlapping clusters of meaning associated with the word. Some uses refer primarily to activities and transactions as in such expressions as 'business as usual', 'any other business', or 'business is brisk'. At other times the idea of business implies certain values and objectives, as when the Confederation of British Industry is said to represent 'business interests'.

Unfortunately, there is no agreement about the exact nature of these interests. Business objectives might be equated with economic objectives. In this case a business organisation might be defined as any organisation whose primary aim was the creation of economic wealth as compared with other organisations with non-economic objectives such as churches, schools or political parties. In other contexts the idea of business implies the production and sale of goods and services for profit by a privately owned enterprise. Under this usage a publicly owned enterprise such as a water authority would not be classed as a business organisation even though its goals are primarily economic.

Nobody would deny the importance of business in the modern world even if we take the more restricted view of business as the private, profit-orientated sector of the economy. Most economic activity is initiated in the private business sector, even in a 'mixed' economy such as that of the UK, but apart from their obvious economic importance, 'business' decisions influence almost every aspect of society — social, moral and political.

In particular, a common theme amongst social commentators is the influence of modern business on cultural and moral values as when Mishan (1967) expresses a widespread concern about the effects of our continual exposure to consumer advertising:

> By drawing attention daily to the mundane and the material, by hinting continually that the big prizes in life are the things that only money can buy, the influences of advertising and popular journalism conspire to leave a man restless and discontent with his lot. These influences, moreover, are rapidly producing a society in which standards of taste and decorum are in a continuous state of obsolescence, leaving fashion alone as the arbiter of moral behaviour. (p.173).

Other writers have taken a more favourable view of the contribution to society of the modern business corporation. For instance, Schon (1971) believes that we have a great deal to learn from the obvious success of business firms in adapting to the rapid changes in society of recent years:

> Business firms in western society have been primary vehicles for the diffusion of innovations and therefore, in a major sense, agents of social learning for society at large. Moreover, seen as a form evolving in relation to its changing environment, the business firm has been unsurpassed over the last fifty years in its ability to effect rapid inventive transformations of itself without flying apart at the seams, without disappearing as a form, often without loss of identity even at the level of the individual firm. (p.61)

Whether for good or ill, the business organisation is a powerful force in modern society. This book is concerned with exploring the rich collection of activities and organisations

which we call business. It looks at the raw material for the
study of business: the individual enterprise with its departments and functions, the environment of the business enterprise, the objectives of the business and the way managers try
to achieve those objectives. Such a feeling for the facts of
business activity might be acquired through many years of
practical experience in positions of responsibility; a textbook
description of these activities is no substitute for this experience.

In an attempt to impart a degree of realism to the subject
we shall rely heavily on a business case history. The many
facets of business activity will be illustrated by reference to
'Small Print Limited' – a company selling machinery and
equipment to the printing industry.

An approach to the study of business through a detailed
case history serves as a timely warning of the risks of excessive
generalisation. There may be similarities between Small Print,
Unilever, Marks and Spencer, and the local newsagent's shop,
but at first sight it is the difference between these units
which stands out most sharply. However legitimate it may be
for the economist to define 'business objectives' or talk about
the cost curves of 'the firm', these discussions can only be
valid within the conventions and rules of economic discourse
and with a full appreciation of the rich diversity behind such
generalisations.

There is a further lesson to be learned from looking at a
detailed case history. No matter how much detail is included
in the case about the firm's history, organisational structure,
product range, financial situation or competitive position,
there is always more information which might be relevant in
helping us to understand the firm's operations. There is an
infinite number of possible 'facts' about any company, real
or imaginary: neither the reader of a business case history nor
a manager faced with a difficult business problem can ever
have perfect knowledge.

Nor is the manager a passive recipient of random items of
information. He will make a selection of those facts which he
perceives as being important for the decision and his perception will depend on a variety of factors including his education,
training, previous experience and psychological traits, the

quality of the firm's information system and the extent of his contacts outside the business. An extract from our case study of Small Print will serve as an illustration:

> In the company's early days, sales were mainly to printers in the UK and so it was decided to base its operations at Watford, a major centre of the printing industry. As the company grew in size, a small factory with office accommodation was leased close to the original office and warehouse. At the present time the rent of the Watford site is high and the premises are overcrowded. Moreover, as 80% of the company's sales are for export the original reason for the Watford location is no longer valid. The directors are therefore considering a proposal that the entire operation of the firm should be transferred to a new site on Merseyside which is a development area and therefore attracts some government grants.
>
> What pieces of information do the directors consider to be most important in helping them arrive at a decision? Mr Porter, the Finance Director, sees the long-term savings from more efficient operations in a purpose-built factory at relatively low rents as the main consideration. Mr Jones, the Administrative Manager, is worried about the severe disruption that will follow from a complete break with the Watford site: 'We would never recover from the chaos! We have managed perfectly well here for nearly twenty-five years — what is the point of changing now?' Mr Smith, the Personnel Manager, sees the effect of the proposed move on the labour force as the critical factor: 'You cannot expect all our scientific and technical staff to move their families to Liverpool at a moment's notice. Would we be able to recruit skilled labour in the area?'

Just as the manager selects those items of information which he perceives to be important when reaching a decision, the writer of a case presents those details which he considers to be significant for an understanding of the business he is describing.* The case study writer's perception is just as selective as that of the manager. In both instances the mind selects from a mass of detail and organises the material into patterns which will give some meaning to the detail.

As the Small Print case history unfolds itself in the following chapters, it will become apparent that there is such a pattern in the presentation. A 'systems' approach will be used to introduce the various functions and activities in the

---

* In order to develop the student's own powers of perception a case study may often be presented deliberately in a more random fashion with a certain amount of irrelevant information rather like 'red herrings' planted in a good detective story.

business. Small Print is subject to economic, social, political and other forces from the world outside; it is not a closed system but exists in a complex and changing environment. To use the language of systems theory: the business enterprise is a complex 'open' system.

The systems perspective focuses our attention on relations between the business and its environment, and between the various sub-systems within the organisation. Systems thinking guards us against seeing problems in terms of the separate departments in the business as isolated units.

Some of the implications of systems theory for the study of business will be considered more fully in the final chapter. At this stage, it is sufficient to recognise the idea as a framework for the presentation of material about Small Print. Chapter 2 introduces the enterprise, Chapter 3 relates the business to its environment, and in Chapter 4 we examine the performance of the enterprise in its environment.

The following chapters look in rather more detail at the major functions of the business: marketing, production, personnel and financial management. Chapter 9 discusses government and the law as major elements in the business environment. In an introductory text it is impossible to do more than skim the surface of these subjects and indicate the problems likely to be encountered by managers in the different areas of business. Detailed discussion of certain problems and methods is included in each chapter to give the flavour of the subject rather than attempt an exhaustive treatment of it. The final chapter considers various strategies and approaches which may be useful in the further study of business behaviour in order to analyse and understand that behaviour and to develop the ability to solve complex business problems. A course of business or management studies will contain many elements and it is often difficult to see how these may be integrated into a coherent whole. This book is therefore dedicated to the proposition that there may well be merit in taking an aerial view of the wood before undertaking a detailed examination of the trees.

CHAPTER 2

The Business Enterprise

Business Organisation

Peter Small was born in London, in 1914. After leaving school, he
worked as a draughtsman for a large engineering company, qualifying
as a mechanical engineer by evening study. After the war, he took a
post as technical sales representative for a medium-sized company
selling engineering products in the UK and abroad. In 1952, he was
asked to become the English selling agent of Cliché, a long-established
French company which manufactured printing machinery of traditional design. As a result of this approach, Peter Small decided to
set up in business as a selling agent. Another agency was gained in
1955 from the German Druck company for an electronic device
which scanned photographic material and so produced etched plates
for printing. This technique was a significant improvement on the
established method of acid bath etching; operating costs were lower
and a better quality picture was produced.

In 1954 Peter Small entered into a partnership agreement with
Norman Brown, an old friend who brought £10,000 capital into the
business. In 1957, however, Brown decided to withdraw from the
partnership and so in the same year, Peter Small registered his business as a private limited company called Small Print Ltd.

By 1958 the company employed a total of 25 salesmen, storemen
and administrators, and had become highly successful as a selling
agency. The Druck agency proved particularly profitable as the UK
has a large number of local newspapers and the electronic scanner
was well-suited to their requirements. Small found that surplus funds
were available and so he and his fellow directors devoted much of
their energies to devising and appraising new products. For instance,
a new idea for a dish-washing machine was considered but the direc--
tors decided that it would call for a manufacturing facility which they
did not possess and knowledge of a market they barely understood.
Consequently, the product idea was sold to a domestic appliance
manufacturer.

The above account of the origins and early history of the firm introduces us to the different forms of business organisation. Peter Small left his salaried employment in 1952 to set up in business on his own account, but as the firm grew in size he found it advisable to abandon his status as a sole trader. In 1954 he entered into partnership with Brown but formed a private limited company when the partnership was dissolved in 1957. From a legal point of view, the main distinction between the sole trader and partnership forms of organisation and a company is that the latter has a legal identity distinct from the individual or individuals who create it. Small Print Limited and Peter Small are separate 'persons' in the eyes of the law even though Peter Small may own almost all the shares in the company.

The main practical advantage of registering as a limited company is that the liability of all shareholders is limited to the amounts they have agreed to contribute to the company's share capital. Once this amount has been received by the company, a shareholder has no further personal liability whatever financial disasters happen to the company. At this stage in its development, Small Print's capital requirements were fairly modest and so it was sufficient to register as a private company, a step which does not require undue formalities and expense. If a private company expands to such an extent that it needs to obtain finance from the investing public at large, as distinct from arranging its finance privately, it would need to be reconstituted as a public company. It could then apply to the Stock Exchange for its shares to be quoted and so made transferable without restriction.

All businesses, large or small, need a clear business policy to guide their activities. In these early years, the policy of the firm was to act as a selling agency for other companies but not to manufacture products itself. As the company expanded, it had to decide whether to continue this policy or to branch out in new directions. The dish-washing machine proposal involved both a change in market and a change in the company's method of operation: from selling agency to manufacturer. The directors believed that this would be too great a change in direction to countenance at this stage. The company's policy was to build on its established connections with the printing industry as will be seen from the next extract:

> In 1962, the company was approached by a young inventor seeking cash backing to develop a computerised approach to typesetting. The manager of the recently established development department acknowledged that this idea was in line with the requirements of the printing industry but there followed five years of costly development by the company before the idea could be marketed. By 1965, a further project, an inexpensive colour scanner, had been developed by the company. It would now be possible for publishers, advertisers and the designers of packaging to buy their own colour printing machines and have full control of the appearance of their product. The directors expected that this new product would be an attractive proposition to many of their existing UK customers and there was potentially a strong export market. Small Print had acquired limited facilities for manufacturing but it lacked an international marketing organisation. An approach to the publishers, Global Inc., resulted in an agreement for Small Print to provide machines for world distribution through a Global Inc. subsidiary.
>
> In 1967, Small Print had gained a further new product for the printing industry: a phototypesetter. The Company was highly profitable but its funds were fully committed. The directors of Small Print agreed that in order to exploit its products fully, the company should seek membership of a multinational organisation. This was achieved in 1969, by the sale of all of the company's shares to the Caxton Group, a multinational corporation based in the USA. Small Print gained access to a world marketing organisation, and to the comprehensive Caxton library of typefaces which would be important for the efficient development of the phototypesetter. Small Print's customers would now have a wider choice of typefaces.

Over a period of seventeen years the firm has progressed from a small one-man business to the subsidiary of a multinational company. The legal status of the organisation changed over time to meet the various financial, technical and marketing pressures which it experienced, particularly during periods of rapid growth. It might have been possible for the company to raise the additional finance required in the late sixties by 'going public' but, as the case shows, there were sound marketing and technical reasons for the course adopted.

Apart from these formal changes in status the firm entered into a number of important long-term relationships with other companies — the agency agreements with Cliché and Druck and the marketing agreement with Global Inc. In addition to the type of agreement found in the case, businesses may enter into a variety of other arrangements including licensing agreements, joint ventures and franchises. The growing complexity of the legal relationships between firms is a feature of modern business.

This brief history of Small Print Ltd leads to a description of the company's activities in 1975. We shall identify in turn a technical system, social system, financial system and information system of the company.

The Technical System

Small Print has three main product groups: (a) phototypesetters, (b) typesetting peripherals, and (c) colour scanners.* Combination of phototypesetters, typesetting peripherals and the necessary interlinking software results in a 'system'. These vary greatly in their complexity and in their price — £400,000 to over £1m. Systems are designed to the requirements of the particular customer: indeed, any basic product may be modified to a customer's operating needs. Customers frequently visit the plant to see the progress of their equipment's assembly.

All the parts used in the firm's products are bought in from outside suppliers. However, the production process is wider than mere assembly and includes the building-up of complex circuit boards, wiring, testing, and the modification of both newly developed products and established products to meet customers' specified operating requirements.

Each production manager receives a monthly schedule from the sales section setting out the production which will be required to meet customer orders and giving delivery dates for each order. For each product in the schedule a computerised listing of the parts which will be required is prepared. In total, some 5,000 different parts, ranging from mini-computers and disc drives, to wire and screws are required. The parts are drawn from the stores, missing parts noted and those sub-assemblies of the product started which may be completed or at least partly finished without the missing parts. Each completed sub-assembly is tested, first visually for missing parts (an electronic test of a sub-assembly with a missing part may destroy the entire component) and then electronically. Final assembly of the product is followed by a testing of functions and a 'soak' testing over several days simulating the actual use of the product in the conditions specified by the customer.

* See Appendix 1 for a brief description of these products.

The production cycle for phototypesetters and scanners is three to four months, for keyboards it is three to four weeks and a 'system' may take up to nine months. Shortage of parts may extend these cycles.

The technical system of a manufacturing business describes how the various inputs of raw materials and component parts are transferred into saleable products. Small Print's technical system may be expressed in the form of a simple flow diagram as in figure 2.1. The actual conversion process has been outlined in some detail to give an idea of the complexity of many technical systems in practice. A full description of the system would also mention the contribution of many different departments and sections of the business such as purchasing, research and development, production planning and control, packaging and transport. The production processes of any business could be similarly described in a flow diagram. The reader may wish to identify the technical systems of other manufacturing businesses such as a steel works, brewery or bakery and 'extractive' enterprises such as a coal mine, farm, or fishing fleet. It should also be remembered that many businesses are concerned with the production of services rather than goods. An insurance company, department store and airline each has its own distinctive technical system. Indeed, it is a feature of most advanced economies that the service sector of industry is expanding more rapidly than manufacturing. Some writers even claim that we are entering the era of 'post industrial society' or 'the service economy'.

In addition to labour, materials and the provision of outside services such as banking and insurance, the production process will also require fixed capital in the form of buildings, plant and equipment, etc. In deciding to adopt a particular production process the managers of the business are by implication making a choice about the relative contribution of each of these elements. For example, a company may decide to manufacture a component on its own premises or it may wish to sub-contract the work to a specialist firm.

It is not possible to define an ideal production system for a particular industry or firm. Obviously, we would expect an oil refinery to be more capital intensive than a shirt factory but there will exist wide variations in the capital/labour ratio

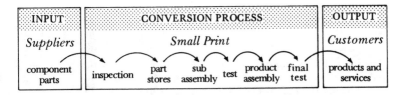

Figure 2.1 Small Print: technical system

between different firms in the same industry. The decision to make a business more or less capital intensive will depend mainly on the relative prices of capital and labour in the economy as a whole. In a developing country such as India where labour costs are low in relation to capital costs we would expect to see more labour-intensive methods of production than in the UK. Over a period of time there has been a tendency to use more capital-intensive methods of production in most industries. A comparison of methods of producing motor cars at the turn of the century with the Ford 'T' model assembly line in the 1920s and modern automated methods of car production is a good illustration of this trend.

The Social System

The technical system of the business which we have just examined cannot be seen in isolation from the men and women who make it function. Although it is convenient to treat the technical and social systems of the business separately the two are so indissolubly linked that many writers prefer to consider the production process as a single 'socio-technical system'.

Table 2.1 gives some information about the composition of the workforce of Small Print in 1975. One striking characteristic is the low proportion of 'direct' production workers employed by the company. It might appear from the figures that only the craftsmen and the operatives, or 31% of the total employees, are actually making anything. However, we should not automatically assume that the other 524 employees are unproductive. Modern industrial production is a

Table 2.1 Small Print: number of employees 1975

	Total	Male	Female
Managers	25	22	3
Scientists and technologists	69	60	9
Sales staff	48	46	2
Technicians and technical engineers	153	153	—
Administrative and clerical	131	30	101
Foremen and supervisors	52	41	11
Skilled craftsmen	80	80	—
Operatives (production)	159	62	97
Labourers and other workers	46	30	16
	763	524	239

complex process requiring the cooperation of many different groups of people if it is to be run efficiently. The clerk in the sales department processing a customer's order and the accountant reporting on a capital investment proposal are contributing to the total production of the company as well as the operative wiring a circuit board. The table shows that Small Print has become a science-based company employing a large number of highly qualified scientists, technologists and technicians to develop new products. The main function of the technical engineers is to help in the installation of new equipment on the premises of customers and provide an after-sales service.

An account of the social system of a business requires much more than a bare statement of the main groups of employees as contained in table 2.1. We are also concerned with *relationships* between members of the business. Many of these relationships arise out of conscious planning, as when a manager receives a detailed job description defining the nature of his responsibilities and duties towards colleagues, subordinates and superiors. This pattern of formal relationships in an organisation is known as its *structure* and this pattern may be conveniently expressed in general terms through an organisation chart. The most recent organisation chart for Small Print is given in figure 4.1. It will be more convenient to defer the detailed discussion of the company's structure until we have introduced the concept of business strategy in Chapter 4. One of the main criteria for assessing the effectiveness of a firm's organisation structure is the extent to which it sets the right climate for meeting the long-range strategic objectives of the business.

An examination of the social system of Small Print will start with its organisation chart but we must remember that these formal relationships cannot give the complete picture. In any social group there are important informal relationships which arise spontaneously out of the activities of the group and are not predetermined by the formal structure. In some cases these informal relationships complement the formal structure; at other times the two may be in conflict, as when a small group of workers establishes a common standard for a 'fair day's work' and brings pressure to bear on the fast worker so that he restricts his output to nearer the group norm.

The Financial System

Having seen something of the company's production process, we must now turn our attention to the way in which all these activities are financed. Materials, labour and outside services are required to maintain the production system and new capital equipment will be required to replace worn-out equipment or to improve the existing methods of production.

All these resources will have to be paid for sooner or later. Money is the medium of exchange in business transactions and so it follows that cash flows will be in the opposite direction to the flow of production which we have described in our examination of the technical system. The delivery of parts from a supplier to the parts store of Small Print will be matched by the cheque in payment — not immediately, as the goods will probably have been bought on credit. Similarly, the customers of the company will eventually settle their accounts for the phototypesetters and colour scanners which have been despatched to them. Figure 2.2 shows this circular flow.

Although the actual flows of money and money's worth are more complex than figure 2.2 would suggest, a comparison with figure 2.1 will show that the company's financial system

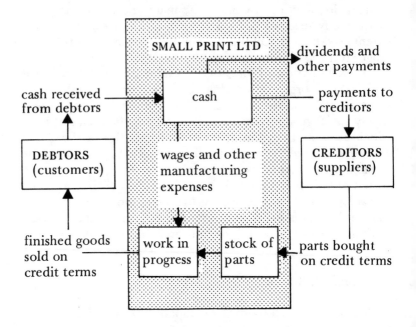

Figure 2.2 Small Print: financial system

is essentially a reflection of the production system expressed in money terms.

Although we need not be concerned with the detailed recording of these flows, it is worth noticing that the relationship between all the accounts in the diagram is similar to that between the inflow and outflow pipes and storage tanks in a plumbing system. Cash is a 'tank' account and its level rises when the cash inflow from debtors and other sources is greater than the cash outflow to creditors, employees and others.

For the business as a whole, it is clearly important for revenue to exceed expenses, in other words, for the business to make a profit. The *income statements* of Small Print (table 8.1) present the figures in some detail over a three-year period. A rearrangement and summarisation of the 1975 figures shows the following position:

Small Print Ltd INCOME STATEMENT for the year ending 30 Sept. 1975 (£'000)

Revenue		
Sales	6,964	
Royalty Income (net)	160	
		7,124
Expenses		
Manufacturing costs		
of goods sold	5,154	
Overheads	1,454	
		6,608
Net Profit before tax		516

The Income Statement records the profit or loss which is generated by flows within the financial system over a period of time. The *balance sheet* shows the level of the assets (e.g. cash, debtors, work in progress and stock) and liabilities such as creditors; it is therefore an indication of the financial position of the business at a particular date. Balance sheets for Small Print over a three-year period are shown in table 8.3. The following is a simplified version of the 1975 balance sheet:

Small Print Ltd BALANCE SHEET as at 30 Sept. 1975 (£'000)

Fixed Assets		
(Buildings, Plant,		520
and Equipment)		
Current Assets		
Stock	1,002	
Debtors	2,726	
Bank and Cash	80	
	3,808	
Less *Current Liabilities*		
(Creditors, Tax and		
Loans owing)	2,739	
Net current Assets		1,069
(working capital)		
Total Net Assets		1,589
Financed by		
Caxton Equity		1,589

As Small Print Ltd is a wholly owned subsidiary of Caxton and there are no long-term loans to the company, the balance sheet shows that the total net worth of the company is financed by Caxton.

The Information System

To an economist there are four basic economic resources or factors of production — labour, capital, land (natural resources) and enterprise (management). Although this classification is valuable in general economic analysis we have seen that it is convenient to adopt a different classification when dealing with an individual business enterprise such as Small Print. We have already seen how the resources of capital, materials, people (workers and management) and outside services are organised and financed. We now turn to a resource which is often overlooked in spite of its importance because it seems intangible and ephemeral compared with the more obvious resources of business — information.

The technical system of Small Print was described in terms of inputs, a conversion process and outputs. Information systems may be analysed in a similar way. The input to the system is the raw data of facts and figures from various sources which is available to the enterprise. In the case of a management information system these data must be converted into reliable information as a basis for effective decision making (figure 2.3).

In the complex and uncertain world of modern business, accurate and prompt information is an important but expensive resource. A growing number of people are employed in the 'knowledge' and 'information' occupations. Within a business organisation we may find clerical workers, computer programmers, accountants, laboratory workers and others whose main task is to process data into information. The firm may also pay for outside produced information as when a market research survey is commissioned from an independent bureau.

It is essential for a science-based company such as Small Print to keep abreast of developments in relevant technologies.

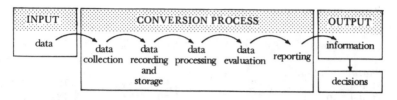

Figure 2.3 Management information system

The company will also need accurate information about the
state of the market and the relative strengths of its competitors. The problems of obtaining information about the
environment of the business will be discussed more fully in
the next chapter. The company also needs information about
its internal activities and so the information system should be
closely related to each of the other major systems of the
business. Personnel, production control and financial information will therefore be prepared for presentation to the
appropriate managers. As accounting reports are an important
source of information for all managers in the business we shall
look at them more closely as an example of internally produced information.

In an accounting information system, data are generated at
each stage of the production process, usually in documentary
form. Purchase orders, goods received notes, requisitions,
despatch notes, invoices and many other documents provide
evidence of the innumerable transactions which go to make
up the firm's activities. These source documents are collected
and the details recorded in the appropriate account. The
processing of these data may be carried out by the traditional
method of posting entries manually; in a firm of any size it is
more likely that accounting machines or an electronic
computer will be used. The skills of the accountant will be
used to summarise and evaluate this information and communicate it in an appropriate manner, usually in the form of
accounting reports.

These accounting statements of the company contain
important information about the company's economic performance. We have already seen simplified versions of a
balance sheet and income statement of Small Print Limited

Table 2.2 Small Print : product sales

Product Lines	72/73		73/74		74/75	
	£'000	%	£'000	%	£'000	%
Phototypesetters						
Model B64	1,682	45.7	1,898	34.5	708	10.2
Model B39	272	7.4	1,308	23.8	3,321	47.7
Typesetting peripherals						
Keyboard	1,282	34.8	1,363	24.8	1,604	23.0
Video terminals	–	–	400	7.3	675	9.7
Colour scanners	275	7.5	323	5.9	446	6.4
All other products	171	4.6	208	3.7	208	3.0
	3,682	100.0	5,500	100.0	6,962	100.0

as examples of such reports. The Companies Acts 1948–1976 require that a copy of these reports, prepared in a prescribed form, must be sent to each shareholder in the company. A further copy must be filed with the Registrar of Companies as part of the annual return which means that the accounts are available for public inspection. The intention is to give shareholders and anyone else with an interest in the company a fair view of its financial state. Recent industrial legislation* also gives workers the right to receive information in the interests of good industrial relations and gives trade unions access to certain types of information which may be valuable in the collective bargaining process.

Apart from this information to shareholders, workers and the public at large, which is prepared to meet the company's statutory obligations, the accountant will also present financial information to management. Whereas shareholders and the general public will require general information about the company's position and profitability, management accounting involves a more detailed analysis of past operations and future prospects. For instance, the figures for total annual sales given in the income statement will need to be analysed to show relative trends between products, and between

* Employment Protection Act 1975 and ACAS Code of Practice No. 2 (1977).

markets; table 2.2 shows that there has been considerable change over the three year period in the demand for different lines although the relative importance of the three main product groups has been more constant.

Within this chapter we have described separately four basic systems which we have chosen to identify in our case study: the technical, social, financial and information systems. It must be emphasised that whatever merit this analysis may have for the purpose of presenting the case material there is an obvious danger in treating these systems in isolation. As will be seen in some of the later chapters of the book, some of the most important problems of business management arise from the interaction between these 'systems'.

In concluding this brief examination of the business enterprise we must recognise another danger. An enterprise is not a 'closed system'; it is related to a complex business environment. In the next chapter we shall continue our analysis of Small Print by looking at the nature of this environment.

CHAPTER 3

The Business Environment

The Concept of the Business Environment

At first sight it seems a relatively easy matter to draw a boundary between the business and its environment, particularly so far as membership is concerned; the law determines whether a given person should be classed as a member of the business or as an outsider. The status of employee and, in a limited company, of shareholder and director, must be defined with some precision because legal rights and duties may depend on whether a particular legal status can be established. For instance, the business is liable for injuries caused by the negligence of an employee acting within the course of his employment, but it is not liable for the wrongs of an 'independent contractor' such as a self-employed window cleaner working on the firm's premises. In law the owners of a company are its shareholders. They may receive dividends, payable out of profits at whatever rate is agreed at the company's annual general meeting. Debenture holders, on the other hand, are outsiders who have made long-term loans to the business and are entitled to interest on their loans whether or not a profit has been made.

Whatever the formal legal position, there is considerable variation in the degree of commitment to the business by different groups of participants in the large business enterprise: directors and senior managers, middle managers, production workers, clerical workers and shareholders. In such a business, the small shareholders have little effective control over the company as individuals, although their collective power may still be important if there is a crisis of confidence in the directors, or if there is a take-over bid from another company. The interest of the small shareholder in the activities of the company is usually limited to the rate of the dividend to be declared.

Many writers on business organisation have commented on this tendency for the control of the large corporation to become separated from its legal ownership; James Burham (1941) even described this shift of power away from share-holders to salaried managers as 'The Managerial Revolution'. In deciding their dividend policy (strictly speaking 'recom-mending' a dividend to the annual general meeting), the directors are for all practical purposes treating the small shareholders as an outside force to be satisfied rather than as active participants in the business. For instance, management plans for ploughing back profits to finance the building of a new factory may have to be reconciled with the need to pay a current dividend which will meet shareholders' expectations. Unless there is the prospect of substantial capital gains on their shares in the future, the shareholders would probably prefer 'jam today' rather than 'jam tomorrow'. So far as the decision about the rate of dividend is concerned, managers will think of the small shareholders as part of the environment.

Although the idea of a boundary between the enterprise and the environment is clear in principle, there is some blurring at the edges when we come to examine the different systems within the business. For instance, the technical systems of many businesses are so clearly linked with those of other businesses that their operation can only be under-stood as an integral part of a larger production system. A farmer under contract to a frozen food company and a garment manufacturer producing to the exact specifications of a large retail organisation are two examples of this close interdependence between businesses which are consecutive links in the production chain. Although each of these smaller units is an independent business in the legal sense, their acti-vities are subject to detailed control by the dominant business organisation in the production chain.

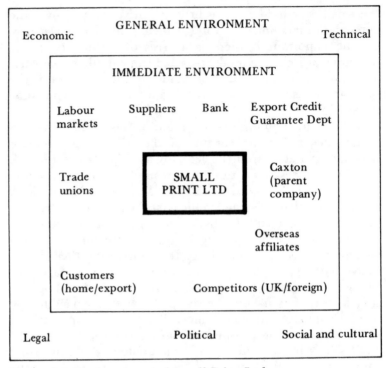

Figure 3.1 Environment of Small Print Ltd

A further ambiguity about boundaries arises when one company is a subsidiary of another. Is Caxton part of Small Print's environment or is Small Print a sub-system of the parent company? The answer depends on how we wish to define the system, but whatever level of analysis is taken it is impossible to ignore the close relationship between parent company and subsidiary.

There are many possible ways of classifying the main sectors of the business environment. As in our discussion of the enterprise itself, the wisest policy is to select the classification which is most appropriate for the task of introducing the Small Print case.

We shall first examine the closest contacts between the enterprise and the outside world. This *immediate environment* includes the markets for the firm's products and markets for the main factor inputs: labour, materials, supplies and finance.

Beyond these immediate contacts the business must be aware of wider economic, technical, political and social developments: these are aspects of its *general environment*. Figure 3.1 illustrates the relationship between these concepts.

The Immediate Environment of Small Print Limited

1. Product Markets

The market for the company's products may be defined as consisting of four segments:

(i) Newspapers —   the weeklies and dailies;

(ii) 'Commercial printers' — magazines, books, catalogues and calendars;

(iii) 'Trade typesetters' — producing plates/films for other firms to print from;

(iv) 'In-plant printers' — large organisations, e.g. I.C.I. and Unilever producing plates/films for their own printing.

Each market requires a different capability in its equipment, e.g. for newspapers — high speed, for books — quality.

The use of electronic typesetting and plate-making equipment results in a considerable lowering of the user's operating costs. These savings are so considerable as to be readily apparent to the prospective customer. Each generation of equipment offers yet lower operating costs, with the effect that customers from five years ago are now beginning to replace their original electronic equipment. In the hope of further savings in their operating costs, customers already employing electronic equipment often urge the equipment manufacturers to make improvements in their products.

Small Print's turnover has for several years been divided 80% to export and 20% to the UK market. The numbers of firms involved in plate-making and typesetting, the availability of funds for investment and the resistance of organised labour (see Chapter 7) are the main factors in determining the strength of any particular market. Although local newspapers in the UK have been buying electronic equipment for a number of years, it is only recently that sales have been made to three UK national newspapers.

The strength of competition varies from product to product. In each segment of the market there are between three to five major competitors. The strongest competition comes from the United States and Germany; there is only one major British firm making printing equipment which is as technically advanced as that of Small Print.

Economists classify markets according to the type of competition which exists between different firms in the market. *Perfect* competition is said to exist in a market containing a large number of firms each one of which has no influence on the selling price of their products. The firms are selling a standard product and there is no competition on quality or service. A farmer faced with a market price for his produce over which he has no control may be said to be operating in a business environment approaching the state of perfect competition.

It is rare to find a pure example of perfect competition in business: a firm will usually try to identify a particular section of the market by differentiating its products from those of its competitors, by the creation of a brand name, a distinctive company image or other devices, and so reduce the random nature of its environment. Where this occurs, a firm is said to be operating in an *imperfect* market. As product differentiation increases, strategic decisions assume greater importance. The managers of the firm will now need to define 'the business we are in' with some precision and to be more conscious of patterns in the business environment. In an imperfect market there are still a sufficiently large number of firms for it to be unnecessary or impractical for any one firm to consider the possible response of rivals to its marketing decisions.

In many markets, a few firms of similar size and importance are in direct competition with each other. This is the economist's *oligopoly,* or a market with a few sellers — the motor car industry, for example. The behaviour of firms in this situation has many similarities with the strategies developed by players in a card game such as solo whist: in both cases there are elements of skill and chance, and a need to anticipate the moves of your opponents in response to your moves. This analogy can be pursued further by applying the 'theory of games' and expressing the 'game' elements in the market behaviour of oligopolists in mathematical form and deriving solutions which may guide the businessman in his choice of strategy.

The concepts of perfect competition, imperfect competition and oligopoly are drawn from the traditional economic theory of markets. The systems theorists, Emery and Trist (1965), have suggested a classification of organisational environments which is more general than an economic classification of markets. Their idea of a *turbulent environment* is of particular interest in our discussion of Small Print. An environment is said to be turbulent when its very nature is changing, possibly as a result of political or social influences as well as economic forces. As in the case of a business operating in an oligopolistic market, other organisations are the dominant feature of the environment but these may also include large trade unions, major suppliers, regulating bodies or even governments (in the oil industry, for example), as well as business competitors. Markets may change rapidly and it is likely that research and development are increasingly important factors in business success. In a turbulent environment, wise strategic decisions and a flexible organisation structure are essential if the firm is to adapt and, indeed, survive in the midst of this change.

With these categories in mind, how should we describe the environment of Small Print? From the small number of business competitors it is clear that the company is operating in an oligopolistic market. The importance of research and development, the short life-cycle of many of the products, the changing balance in the various segments of the market, and the political instability of some of the export markets are also indications of turbulence. Whether this means that we should place the environment of Small Print in Emery and Trist's 'turbulent' category is a matter of debate. In any case, the classifications of economists and systems theorists are intended for purposes of analysis only; in the real world the environment of an organisation, particularly of a multi-product business, will exhibit elements of more than one type.

2. Labour

The composition of the labour force of Small Print Limited has already been given (table 2.1). At the moment the rate of turnover is low amongst most groups of workers. It is highest amongst female clerical workers (many leave for better paid posts in central London), and amongst operatives. In recent years the company has experienced difficulty in recruiting skilled fitters and electronic inspectors. It has also been difficult to find supervisory staff with experience of production systems similar to those in operation at Small Print.

When two senior development posts were advertised recently there was a large number of highly qualified applicants, but few with any experience of 'modification technology'. Both posts were therefore filled by internal promotions.

There is not a single labour market for the skills required by the company but several distinct markets. Small Print is a science-based company operating in a specialised market. It will have highly specific requirements in terms of skills and experience for certain positions in the business and so it may be virtually impossible to 'buy in' these skills on the open market. This points to the need for a properly planned training scheme for the development of this expertise.

3. Suppliers

Such items as computers, disc systems, display units, paper tape punches, CRT systems and magnetic tape systems, are supplied by large companies, who are often the main producers of a particular type of component. Other specialist firms supply the smaller parts. Few parts are ordered to Small Print's specifications; the technique generally employed is to modify the bought-in parts whenever this is necessary to meet the design requirements of the final product.

The computer provides a monthly check upon deliveries. In periods of economic growth, the suppliers of electronic components frequently over-commit themselves and fail to meet promised delivery dates.

Small Print undertakes to service all its products. While current equipment may be serviced by 'raiding' the production stores, a further 4,000 different parts are held in store to service discontinued models. None of these parts are employed in current production and the service stock records are not computerised. In monetary terms, service stock has doubled in the last two years. No means of determining an optimum level for this stock has been found. Most of the electronics are only five years beyond their introduction, and are consequently without an established failure rate.

We have already considered the contribution of the individual business firm as part of a wider production system, when discussing boundaries between the enterprise and its environment. This high degree of interdependence between business units is a feature of modern industrial organisation, and is illustrated most vividly when a labour dispute in a car components factory has repercussions throughout the entire motor industry. In a simple economy, production is often directly for the consumer as in the case of a village carpenter. Recent proposals for the adoption of 'alternative technologies' may be seen in part as a move towards simpler and less interdependent methods of production.

There is often a long chain from the extraction of raw materials to the sale of the finished product to the consumer. The links in this chain are productive processes such as mining, refining, manufacturing, assembling, packaging, storing, transporting, distributing or selling. At each stage value is added, and the raw materials are gradually transformed into a product which is made available for sale to the ultimate consumer at a time and place that suits his requirements. Each business enterprise makes its own contribution by forging one or more links in this chain of production.

Small Print's 'distinctive competence' is to take standard products from their suppliers, modify and assemble them into specialised products and design-related computer programmes or 'software' for direct sale to an industrial market. The company must have an understanding of the basic technology of these parts in order to follow the policy with success. This position could be contrasted with the supply of components in the car industry, for example, where the car manufacturer usually lays down precise specifications for the components without necessarily having a detailed knowledge of the suppliers' technology.

4. Finance

Small Print Limited is a fully owned subsidiary within the Caxton group. The policy of the group is to allow subsidiaries to retain the profits they have earned by not requiring the remittance of a dividend to the parent company provided a good case can be made out for these retentions. If any additional finance is required the subsidiary may make arrangements within its own country or apply for a loan from the parent company at current market rates. In the case of Small Print, short-term finance is available from the bank, and as a high proportion of the company's business is for export, the help of such agencies as the government-sponsored Export Credit Guarantee Department is of particular importance.

In order to show the sources of the funds used by the company the accountant has prepared a cash flow statement (table 3.1). Finance may be obtained by ploughing back

Table 3.1 Small Print: CASH FLOW STATEMENT between 1 Oct. 1974
and 30 Sept. 1975 (£'000)

Sources of cash

Net profit before tax	516	
Increase in creditors	785	
Increase in tax liability	18	
Increase in loans	557	
		1876

Utilisation of Cash

Purchase of fixed assets	109	
Tax paid	179	
Increase in debtors:		
Home customers	591	
Overseas affiliates	770	
Increase in stocks	239	
		1888
Decrease in cash during year		−12

profits, by borrowing new funds or by increasing short-term
liabilities to creditors and others. These funds may be used to
increase current assets such as stocks, debtors and cash, to
make payments of dividends or taxation, or to purchase new
fixed assets such as plant and machinery.

From the cash flow statement, it appears that the level of
profit earned is not sufficiently high to finance the current
operations of the company, and that a considerable increase
in short-term borrowing (including extended credit from
suppliers) has been necessary. It should be remembered that
Small Print has not been required to pay any dividend to the
parent company. Normally this item would be a further call
on the cash resources of a company, but in spite of this
favourable position Small Print has been forced to increase its
short-term debt.

The General Environment

The distinction between the immediate and the general
environment of a business cannot be precise. The relative
importance of different features of the environment may

change over time. Beyond the business's immediate competitors and suppliers of resources there is a progression of wider interests — industry, national economy and international economy. The firm's relations with particular interest groups such as trade unions, employer associations and trade associations must be seen in the wider context of policies agreed nationally with the TUC or the CBI.

An understanding of the economic environment of business must start with a discussion of industrial structure. It is usual to divide industries into three main groups: primary (agriculture, mining and fishing), secondary (including gas, water, electricity and construction) and services (public, personal and commercial). When assessing a potential export market, Small Print would be able to obtain a rough, general assessment of the economy by looking at the national income per head of the population and the proportions of the total workforce employed in the three main sectors. Table 3.2 shows the relevant figures for the UK.

Table 3.2 UK employment analysed by industrial sector

	primary	——secondary——		——service——			Total in employ-ment
			other				
		manu-	produc-	public	other		
	extractive	facturing	tion	services	services	Total	
	%	%	%	%	%	%	
1961	7	36	8	14	35	100	23.2m
1971	4	34	9	17	36	100	23.9m
1981*	3	31	9	21†	36	100	25.0m

Source: Department of Employment Gazette, May 1975, pp. 400-5.
* Projected figures
† These estimates were made before the various plans to curb public spending were announced in 1975—1977.

The proportion employed in the service sector has been increasing at the expense of primary production and manufacturing. Similar trends may be observed in most developed economies many of which have more than 50% of the working population in service industries.

The company's market research specialists will analyse in some detail the demand for the company's own products and those of its competitors. They may also be interested in trends within the industry in general. Table 3.3 shows the total investment by the paper, print and publishing industry in the UK and so gives some idea of the growth of the 'printing machinery industry' of which Small Print is a part. The table also shows progressively higher aggregates of investment until we reach the figures for gross domestic product (the total value of goods and services produced in the UK during a year). The connection between the demand for Small Print's products and some of these higher aggregations may appear somewhat remote but a knowledge of trends in different sectors of the economy is important in strategic planning.

To the government, however, reliable information about national income, employment, production, exports, imports, etc., is essential if its economic policies are to meet with any success. Government economic decisions will have a considerable bearing on such matters as credit availability, levels of inflation, business confidence and levels of employment. Managers will have to take all these matters into account when formulating business plans.

> Because about 80% of Small Print's products are exported, the company will be particularly interested in political and economic developments abroad. 15% of exports were to Eastern European countries, negotiations being mainly conducted through state agencies. 30% of exports were to Middle East countries and here the main concern was political stability. There had been a growing business with companies in the Lebanon until the civil war of 1975/76. About 5% of sales were to less developed countries where major difficulties were poor communications, weaknesses in the industrial superstructure and lack of suitably trained staff for maintenance.

It is apparent that a company with such a high proportion of exports is likely to have a more complex environment than one concentrating its efforts on the home market. Small Print will need to be sensitive to customs, attitudes and business practice in overseas markets where these matters are taken for granted when dealing with home customers. Products have to be modified to meet local markets. A particular problem faced by the company with its high stake in Middle East markets has been the design of computer programmes to deal with material in Arabic.

Any attempt to give a complete list of all aspects of the environment which affect business decisions would be futile.

Table 3.3 Proportion of UK national income attributable to investment at increasing levels of aggregation (£m)

UK national income at market prices	*1971*	*1972*	*1973*	*1974*	*1975*
Investment (gross domestic capital formation) in plant and machinery:					
(a) paper, printing and publishing industries	90	87	121	147	146
(b) total manufacturing industries	1,677	1,543	1,803	2,294	2,574
(c) all industries	3,938	4,007	5,854	5,664	6,652
Investment (gross domestic capital formation) in all types of assets, all industries.	10,515	11,680	14,148	16,633	20,510
Gross domestic product	56,944	63,095	72,089	81,859	103,286

Source: National Income and Expenditure 1965−75, Central Statistical Office, 1976

The business enterprise has been called the representative institution of modern industrial society, and as such it influences and is influenced by every aspect of that society. Even to classify the business environment into its component parts means creating many artificial distinctions. In their day by day activities businessmen are concerned with a multitude of events in the outside world; it matters little to them whether these influences are labelled economic, social or political. It is usual to assume that business profit is created as a result of economic transactions between the enterprise and its environment, but profitability may also be affected by 'political' action such as pressure to impose import controls to prevent 'dumping' by foreign competitors, and legal action to protect the company's patent rights. Government regulation of monopolies and restrictive practices is another area where the economic, political and legal categories merge. With these warnings in mind the reader should examine table 3.4 which lists some connections between broad social and cultural factors, and various 'business' considerations such as consumer demand, attitudes to business and the availability of skilled labour. This is a wide area and two illustrations must suffice to show the importance of these connections.

Drawing on historical evidence of growth in a variety of different societies and periods, McClelland (1961) claimed that there is a connection between the course of economic history and the intensity and distribution of a psychological drive — 'the need for achievement'. For instance, England in the eighteenth century was an 'achieving society' and it was the motivation of key groups such as the early factory owners which provided the driving force for the Industrial Revolution, as much as economic factors (the availability of cheap credit) and demographic factors (the rapid rise of population). The theory is a further illustration of the danger of placing 'economic', 'social' and 'psychological' variables in watertight compartments.

The industrial system is dependent on the education system for its supply of trained manpower. Complex technology requires highly trained 'technocrats' to manage the production process: engineers, marketing men, accountants, research

Table 3.4 Social/cultural environment of business

	Characteristics		Influences on the business environment
Social	Social structure, e.g. social class and social mobility Family patterns Occupational structure Level of industrialisation Social disturbance, e.g. 'alienation'		
Cultural	Ideologies and belief systems, e.g. religion Values and norms, e.g. attitudes to science and technology attitudes to occupations including professions attitudes to economic growth Leisure patterns Mass media – patterns of communication		Patterns of consumer expenditure Size and skills of labour force Status of science and technology Attitudes to business
Demographic	Population: age and sex distribution size and rate of growth geographic distribution urban concentration		
Educational	Structure of the educational system Level of basic literacy Proportion receiving higher education		

scientists. Skilled craftsmen and technicians are also needed in large numbers. As industrial demands for these skills increase, the educational system becomes more closely linked to business.

The Role of Government

One of the most striking features of the modern business environment is the increasingly important role of government. A business may try to reduce the amount of uncertainty in its environment by such devices as taking over a key supplier in order to secure its sources of raw materials, increasing the level of self-financing by ploughing back a high proportion of its profits and the manipulation of consumer demand by advertising. There will still remain many areas of uncertainty which are outside the control of even the largest of corporations. To what extent does the state undertake to reduce this uncertainty by the regulation of total demand in the economy, economic planning or other forms of intervention?

In command economies such as the Soviet Union the answer is straightforward. The state takes the initiative in all economic activity of any importance. This role implies a considerable degree of economic planning to coordinate production and relate it to consumer demands and political goals. We have seen that for sales to Eastern European countries Small Print deals directly with state buying agencies. There is considerable difference between this authoritarian planning of an economy as practised in some communist countries and the 'indicative planning' favoured in parts of Western Europe. In a private enterprise system economic activities are promoted by individual business firms. However, it is difficult to imagine such a system existing in its pure form under modern conditions. The British economy for instance is usually described as a 'mixed' system with the government regulating total economic demand, controlling business activity in a number of directions and often taking an independent economic initiative.

The business firm may therefore be seen as one of a number of agencies making economic decisions. Scarce factors of production such as labour, capital and natural resources are bought at the market rate and converted into goods and services which it is hoped will satisfy the economic wants of potential consumers. The business firm is usually distinguished from other economic agencies by the profit motive; without the prospect of profit, businessmen would be unwilling to undertake the risks of economic innovations. It is not necessary to accept the assumption of classical economic theory that the firm will try to *maximise* profit. It is sufficient to accept that in the long term some level of profit is a necessary condition for survival of the private business.

Many writers would take the argument an important step further and claim that the market mechanism with the profit motive as the main spur to economic initiative is the most efficient system yet devised for allocating economic resources. State planning is bound to be clumsy compared with the fine balancing of supply and demand which is achieved by the 'invisible hand' of market forces.

One conclusion from this line of reasoning is that the role of the state should be limited to the 'nightwatchman' functions of law and order, defence and foreign policy. This extreme 'laissez-faire' position was in fact never advocated by any of the major early political economists and modern versions of the doctrine allow a significant role for the state. For instance, control of monopolies and other 'distortions' of the pure market economy are usually justified as proper areas for state intervention. This extension is perfectly logical if we agree that the free play of market forces will maximise what is considered to be the total economic welfare of a society. Given the assumption that firms will continue production up to that level of output which gives the maximum possible profit out of any market situation, it can be shown as a piece of deductive reasoning that a monopolist will restrict output below what would be produced if there were instead a large number of evenly matched firms competing in the industry. Monopolies, price agreements and other devices for limiting the free play of the forces of competition are therefore aberrations which need to be controlled by the state if the market system is to yield the true benefits which are claimed for it.

Others would justify state initiative in those areas of advanced technology where market uncertainties, high research costs and long development periods make it unlikely that private risk capital would be available. Even in the United States which is often assumed to be the heartland of the free enterprise system there can be few areas of high technology which are entirely free from state support in one form or another. The close connection between defence and advanced technology is one reason for this involvement but as in the case of atomic energy, it is often difficult in practice to distinguish between the military and domestic implications of basic research. To these reasons of military strategy may be added arguments about economic strategy as for instance in the desire of the British to retain an independent computer industry.

Even wider extensions to the role of the state are implied if social as well as economic and political objectives are allowed. The strict doctrine of the market implies that only those firms able to operate efficiently and meet consumers' needs will make profits and so continue in business. Unfortunately, survival of the fittest also implies extinction of the weakest. This can seem a harsh rule and governments are under constant pressure to temper its application in particular cases. The prospect of high unemployment in coal mining areas and fear of over-reliance on imported fuels may mean that the tendency to substitute other fuels for coal is delayed as a result of government policies. In most countries the prices of farm products are supported by a variety of devices aimed at protecting the farming community from the full blast of market forces and encouraging certain types of food production. Home industries may be protected from cheap foreign competition by tariffs, quotas and other important restrictions. In a period of inflation governments may seek to regulate incomes and prices and so damp down the market forces which may be one cause of the inflation.

Faced with such bewildering collections of special cases the cynic may perhaps be excused for asking whether there is in fact any sector of the economy which is still subject to free market forces in the strict sense. However, it is still possible to argue that in spite of these interventions the market is still the dominant force in the economy. Although we may regulate or modify market forces, they will reassert themselves in the long run and we ignore their operation at our peril. A good example of this line of reasoning is in the March 1973 report of the Select Committee on Nationalised Industries which criticised the government for forcing the British Steel Corporation to set artificially low steel prices and so starve itself of funds for future capital expansion.

Modern writers in this tradition of economic liberalism are also concerned with another consequence of their faith in the power of the market to distribute resources more efficiently than state planning. The idea that politicians and civil servants should stick to government also implies that businessmen should stick to business. Writers such as F.A. Hayek (1960) and Milton Friedman (1963) are highly critical of the tendency of modern corporations to define their objective in social as well as economic terms. The concern of some company directors and management theorists with the social responsibilities of business — 'the soulful corporation' as it has been called — is viewed by Hayek and Friedman with suspicion. In their view, the over-riding social goal of business is to make profits. Other objectives will only blur the main issue, lead to inefficient distribution of resources and encourage governments and other groups in society more properly concerned with social responsibility to shirk their responsibilities.

We shall return to the theme of the relationship between industry and government in more detail in Chapter 9. In particular, we shall look more closely at the function of the law in the regulation of business activities in the UK.

Information about the Environment

In order to detect and assess trends in the environment, the company will need an information system, or a set of related information systems each concerned with a part of the environment. We shall be considering the marketing information system of Small Print in Chapter 5. Market research information will help to control the operation of the marketing system on a day-to-day basis. It is also essential if the firm is to make wise strategic decisions such as whether to diversify into a new range of products. The directors of the company will also need to keep abreast of general economic, political, legal and industrial relations developments. In practice the company relies heavily on the foreign department of its bank to provide an information service about its export markets.

A science-based company such as Small Print must be aware of the latest technical developments in order to improve existing products and develop new ones. Its components suppliers are particularly important as a source of technical information.

The quality of information about changes in environment is clearly important if the business is to make effective decisions. Managers may obtain this information from personal sources (customers, suppliers, superiors, subordinates) or from impersonal sources (company reports, publications, official statistics, etc.). In his study, *Scanning the Business Environment*, Aguilar (1967) found that in practice impersonal sources were much less significant than personal sources. Production managers relied heavily on suppliers, and marketing managers relied heavily on customers for their information. Informal networks for passing on information were often more important than the official 'system' which a company had established for scanning the environment.

Many of the companies surveyed by Aguilar were particularly weak at obtaining information which would be relevant for long-range strategic planning. As we shall see in the next chapter, the increasing pace of change in the business environment means that strategic decisions are assuming more significance. The task of devising appropriate strategic information systems must be a matter of urgency if a company is to be able to adapt to these changes.

CHAPTER 4

Business Performance: Strategy and Organisation

In our discussion of the business enterprise (Chapter 2) and its environment (Chapter 3), we have so far been content to describe business in some detail without paying much attention to the purpose of all this activity. In the present chapter we shall try to show the business in action — to bring the picture to life as it were. What should be the long term objectives of the business? Are current operations being conducted efficiently? Does the present organisation meet future strategic needs?

Writers on business policy draw a distinction between three different types of business decisions — strategic, structural and operational. *Strategic decisions* relate to the business's long-term objectives and goals. For example, should the company diversify into other lines of business? Should the business expand by internal growth or by taking over other companies? *Structural or administrative decisions* are concerned with organising the human resources in such a way that the company is likely to realise its potential and meet its strategic objectives. Decisions about the business's day-to-day activities in such fields as production, marketing and purchasing are classed as *operational decisions*.

There is a clear logical sequence connecting these three types of decision. A business should first settle its strategic objectives and then design an appropriate organisational structure in order to meet those objectives and control its detailed operations. Strategic intentions should be carried out through operational plans. In the above statements, the word 'should' is important. Unfortunately, this is not necessarily an account of what actually happens in business enterprises. Many businesses do not concern themselves with strategy and are only forced to change direction in response to an imminent crisis such as a dramatic fall in demand for their products. In others the organisational structure has grown more by historical accident than by conscious planning. The need to tackle the immediate operational problems such as the customer pressing for delivery, means that the more fundamental issues of strategy and structure are often ignored.

The three types of decisions should be related therefore to the long-term objectives of the company. As the word implies, an 'objective' should if possible be expressed in precise measurable terms, and should relate to the position at some future date. 'The company will achieve a 25% share of the market for colour scanners by 1980' is a valid objective whereas 'The company strives to manufacture a high quality product at a reasonable profit' is too vague to serve as a practical statement of objectives.

We shall, therefore, first consider business objectives before turning to the strategic, structural and operating decisions which face the business.

Objectives

Some writers would dispute the validity of ascribing goals to a business on the grounds that, although people can have goals, organisations cannot form intentions about their future actions. The managing director may have a plan for the growth of the company over the next few years and the plan may have been agreed by a committee of senior managers, but it is only by use of a convenient fiction that the plan may be called 'company policy'. Although the company is a 'legal person' it cannot have all the attributes of a natural person. 'A corporation has neither a body to be kicked nor a soul to be damned.' In practice the courts avoid this difficulty by assuming that the company is able to act through certain individuals. The actions of these individuals are imputed to the company itself. For instance, the directors and other employees acting as *agents* are able to enter into binding contracts on behalf of the company provided such agreements are within the company's powers. In criminal law it is usually necessary to provide evidence of an act of will or a state of mind in order to prove a particular crime. In some criminal cases the courts are prepared to 'lift the veil of corporate personality' and see what was in the minds of those representatives of senior management who may be presumed to be taking decisions on behalf of the company.

In managerial economics as in company law, it is sometimes necessary to go behind the legal fiction of the company to find out who makes the decisions. Cyert and March (1963) define the objectives of the business as those which emerge from the 'dominant coalition' of senior managers and others who are in a position to guide the firm's strategy.

Even if it is legitimate to speak about the objectives of the business, there is still disagreement about what those objectives should be. Traditional economic theory assumes that a firm will arrange its affairs so as to maximise profit. More recent writers have tried to refine this theory by suggesting that the firm will maximise sales, net worth or some other function or combination of functions. Given the complexity of its operation, a high degree of uncertainty and the lack of complete information about its activities, should the business be content with a *satisfactory* level of profit rather than trying to *maximise* profit or some other variable? Is there a conflict between short- and long-term economic objectives? To what extent should non-economic objectives be followed?

Many companies will lay down a basic economic objective and then work out the implications of this major objective for the various functional areas of the business.

Small Print is a member of the Caxton group which has defined the basic economic objectives of all companies within the group as follows:

(1) a minimum increase of 10% a year in earnings per share averaged over a five year period.

(2) new products should achieve a return on investment equal to or greater than 20%.

Table 4.1   Small Print: business objectives 1975

A. Physical goals

1. Market standing	To achieve a 10% share of the world market for colour scanners by 1978.
2. Products	(a) To increase the proportion of 'system sales' to 25% of total sales by 1978.
	(b) To increase technical compatibility between the firm's products.
3. Innovation	To introduce new products only if they satisfy certain criteria as to profit margins, return on capital employed, and compatibility with the rest of the firm's product range.
4. Profitability	(a) To install a cost reduction programme with a target of 5% of the cost of goods sold in any one year.
	(b) Prices to be reviewed quarterly and adjusted in accordance with current rates of inflation.
	(c) To conduct a systematic review of all products with a gross profit margin of less than 25%, followed by appropriate action, e.g. drop the product, redesign for higher profit, or replace with a new product.

An individual company within the group such as Small Print is required to formulate a coherent set of goals which will form the basis of its long-term strategy. These goals must then be translated into specific objectives, preferably in quantitative form, which state what the company hopes to achieve by a certain time. Table 4.1 gives an indication of some of the objectives which might be set for the directors of Small Print if it is to meet the basic economic objectives laid down by the Caxton group. The particular classification of physical and relationship goals used in this example was suggested by Denning (1968). Other classifications are possible and the reader may wish to extend the list of objectives to cover other aspects of the firm's activities such as control of the sales force, proportion of home to export sales, advertising, development costs and public relations.

5. Productivity	(a) To reduce the length of production cycles by an average of 10%.
	(b) To reduce materials wastage by 5%.
6. Physical and financial resources	(a) To conduct a systematic review of purchasing policies under the following headings:
	(i) range of existing suppliers
	(ii) reliability, (quality and delivery record) of existing suppliers
	(iii) purchasing contracts
	(iv) discount policies
	(b) To reduce the average period of credit given to customers to 80 days.

B. Relationship goals

1. Management performance and development	To install a system of 'management by objective' and an improved method of reporting results to managers.
2. Labour force	To reduce the labour rate of turnover among operatives by 10%.
3. External	To extend the role of the market research group to include regular reporting of trends in the business environment to the policy-making group of directors.

Strategy

Ansoff (1965) has defined the strategic problem as 'deciding what business the firm is in and what kinds of business it will seek to enter' (page 18). It may seem that the first of these questions is somewhat naive; Small Print Limited is a manufacturer of printing machinery, the British Shoe Corporation makes shoes, and the Prudential sells insurance. However, the need to define the 'business we are in' with greater precision often draws attention to possible new products or markets which the firm should consider if it wishes to meet its long-term objectives. Failure to do so may result in what Levitt (1960) has called 'marketing myopia'.

Schon (1971) gives us an example — the idea of the 'industry for keeping us in clean clothes'. Textile manufacturers

and retailers, soap and chemical companies, appliance manufacturers, laundries and laundrettes are usually classified as
belonging to separate industries, but it is possible to identify
a separate business system for 'keeping us in clean clothes'
from a pattern of relationships between elements of these
industries. As soon as a firm redefines its role as being in
'clean clothes' rather than 'textiles', new business possibilities
become clear. Home dry-cleaners and disposable clothes are
only two of the new product ideas which may now be considered.

What business is Small Print in? We might suggest five
possible definitions depending on whether the firm takes a
narrow or wider view of its activities:

(1) phototypesetters, typesetting peripherals and colour
scanners
(2) printing equipment using advanced technology
(3) printing equipment
(4) modification and assembly of electronic equipment
(5) advanced technology

The first of these possible definitions is obviously too
narrow and the fifth too wide for practical purposes. The
middle three definitions immediately suggest a number of
alternative new products which the firm could develop if it
decides to adopt a strategy of product development or
diversification.

In evaluating a proposed new strategy, Ansoff suggests that
there should be a 'common thread' between the present business and the proposed product—market position, so that the
direction to be followed by the firm is clear to management
and outsiders alike. Before examining a number of possible
strategies for Small Print let us see how Mr Jones, the hardware development manager, assesses the current situation:

> Small Print and its competitors work within the computer technology
> of their parts suppliers. The basic components as bought from these
> suppliers are modified and assembled to meet the requirements of
> a rapidly changing market. The benefits of a modification strategy
> are substantial: a low use of funds and development staff, a high
> turnover of projects, and some assurance that new products will be
> technically sound and acceptable to the market. Such advantages
> are widely appreciated within the company, allowing expenditure

on development to be limited to 8—10% of turnover. Product development in most rival companies is more fundamental in approach but it is also a more costly and lengthy process.

However, Mr Jones believes that Small Print's development strategy has drawbacks. The use of parts from different suppliers means that problems of compatibility frequently arise. Often these can only be satisfactorily resolved after the product has been installed. Compatibility problems frequently require several visits by service engineers and involve considerable expense in the case of overseas sales. There is also an adverse effect on customer relations. While the customer invariably receives the newly-developed system by the agreed date, final payment is often delayed until the system has been 'debugged' by the service engineers.

At a recent trade fair, Mr Jones viewed with concern the simple, rationalised, yet effective, systems of his competitors — at a lower price than comparable Small Print systems. Nevertheless, with such developments as the application of laser technology, Small Print clearly possesses a range of products in advance of most of its competitors from a technological point of view.

From what we know of Small Print, we are now in a position to list some of the possible strategies which the firm might adopt, and consider how each relates to the firm's current position.

(1) Market Penetration

This strategy involves expansion of the existing market through the same or similar products. Sales and development effort would be directed to selling more of what is being sold at present, improving its design and producing it more efficiently.

(2) Market Development

In this case the present range of products would be sold to new customers. A large part of the company's past development has been of this type, and so the company now serves a wide range of somewhat diverse types of customers: local and national newspapers, large and small commercial printers, in-plant printing departments and trade typesetters. At the moment the in-plant market is relatively underdeveloped.

Small Print could develop its range of low price scanners and make a determined effort to meet the special requirements of this segment of the market. Many businesses have prospered by concentrating their attentions on a specialist section of the market in this way.

(3) Product Development

This seems to be the favoured strategy by the directors of Small Print. The relatively short product life-cycle forces the company to anticipate the changing requirements of their customers, and has led the firm to accept a 'modification strategy' as the most flexible approach. Within this broad policy a number of variations are possible. Should development be concentrated on bringing out a single more compatible range, or should the company continue to develop products to meet special needs as they arise without much thought for compatibility. There is a trade-off here between rationalisation and flexibility.

A further, although rather unlikely possibility, would be to capitalise on the company's relationships with the printing trade, to sell a more diverse range of equipment, becoming in effect a general wholesaler for printing machinery.

(4) Diversification

Diversification involves producing new products for new markets. In some cases 'the common thread' between the existing and the proposed position may still be present. If the firm adopts a policy of vertical integration for instance, the company might buy out one or more of its component suppliers, so that the firm becomes its own customer. This may be done to secure regularity in the supply of those components, or the intention may be to achieve a dominant position in the industry by controlling a large section of the production chain. The example given above is of 'backward' vertical integration. 'Forward' vertical integration occurs when a business wishes to control activities further along the chain of production as when a manufacturer controls his retail outlets. The 'tied houses' controlled by breweries are a well-known example. In the case of Small Print, 'forward vertical integration' would involve the purchase of a printing firm — a most unlikely strategy.

Other instances of diversification would be even more distant from the firm's present position. The technological expertise of the company might be harnessed to new products/markets, such as the numerical control of machine tools or calculating machines. The reader will remember that in the early days of the company, a proposal for a dish-washing machine was rejected on the grounds that it was unrelated to the technical and marketing skills of the company at that time. Most of the examples of diversification suggested above would mean radical changes for the company and it is difficult to see how they are feasible propositions in view of its current financial position. Long-term finance from the parent company would be required.

Structure

Having determined the appropriate strategy for reaching its objectives, the directors must now plan an administrative structure to enable the company to realise its potential.

> The importance of development to the continuing success of Small Print had long been recognised throughout the company. An essential ingredient for successful development is provided by the continuing close liaison between the technical director and the sales director. Through this liaison the evolving requirements of the customer are translated into project specifications for the hardware and software development sections.

This extract brings out clearly the importance of personal relationships in the success of any business enterprise. In a relatively small business it may be possible to rely on informal contacts between managers and other key personnel, without much regard for formal structures. With growing size it becomes necessary to define relationships more precisely.

Various factors influencing organisational structure have been suggested including size, technology and the nature of the environment, or possibly a combination of these factors. There is no 'best' type of organisation, and careful thought needs to be given to the design of an appropriate structure. Failure to do so will create stress and insecurity amongst the members of the organisation, lead to inefficiency in its day-to-day operations, and leave the company ill-equipped to respond to major changes in its environment.

The design of any complex organisational structure has to reconcile two needs which at first sight seem to pull in opposite directions: the need for differentiation and the need for integration. In order to reap the full benefits of division of labour, different specialist activities must be organised separately. The most obvious way of achieving this differentiation is through specialist departments. In Small Print the separate departments are defined in terms of functions (purchasing, personnel, service engineering) or products (photosetters, peripherals, scanners). In some businesses it may also be necessary to define departments in terms of geographical location.

In addition to this differentiation through departments, the organisation has also a vertical division of labour as may be seen from the different levels of authority shown in the organisation chart (figure 4.1). The highest level in the chart which might be termed the 'directorate' with the managing director as 'the first amongst equals' is mainly concerned with policy making and the coordination of the total activities of the business. At the next level the managers are responsible for the execution of policy as it affects the specialised functions and product groups of the business. Within the product groups (photosetters, peripherals, scanners) there are other levels of authority with first-line supervisors responsible for small groups of production workers. In some organisations it may be thought necessary to establish a hierarchy with many more levels than in our example. This is clearly necessary where there is a complex group or divisional structure, but even in a single unit it may be desirable to create additional levels if one manager would otherwise have to coordinate the activities of a large group of subordinate managers.

Having seen how the activities of the business are differentiated horizontally through departmentalisation and vertically through the hierarchy, we must now discuss how these activities may be coordinated so that the business acts as an

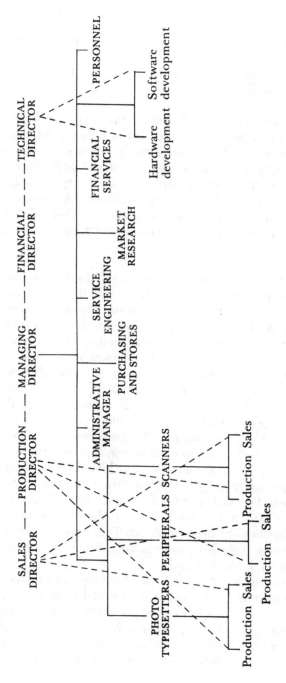

Figure 4.1 Small Print: organisation chart, January 1975

integrated whole. This in its turn implies an understanding of the relationships between different managers in the organisation. In the Small Print case at least three such relationships may be identified.

(1) Line relationships shown by thick vertical lines in the chart. These relationships are clearly between superiors and subordinates. A subordinate is made responsible for a certain part of the business's activities, and should be given sufficient authority to be able to carry out these responsibilities. A superior controls and coordinates the work of his subordinates, who will in their turn supervise the work of subordinates under their control. Coordination is achieved through the hierarchy.

(2) Staff relationships as shown by the dotted lines between the production and sales directors, and the production and sales sections of the three product group departments, indicate responsibility for the supply of advice and services as distinct from the general control which is implied by a line relationship. The complexity of modern business operations means that no one person can specialise in all aspects of management, and so functional specialists may share these responsibilities with the line managers, so far as their particular specialism is concerned. The exact nature of this type of relationship depends on the circumstances. In some cases a specialist will act as an adviser to another manager, but will not have any responsibility for that manager's actions. The sales manager for the phototypesetter product group may call upon the services of the market research team, although the market researchers are not responsible for the use made of the information which they produce. The authority of a staff adviser stems from his professional competence rather than his status in the hierarchy.

The growing importance of staff advisers and managers in modern business is, of course, connected with the need to make use of the contributions of many different specialists in solving complex business problems. New forms of technology require new organisational structure if these complex activities are to be properly integrated, as may be seen in the project management teams set up for advanced technological projects such as manned space flights.

(3) Horizontal relationships between colleagues. In Small Print horizontal relationships are likely to be as important as the vertical line management relationships. Discussions in formal committee may be supplemented by informal meetings between managers and by special working parties set up as the need arises. For instance, a weakness in the design of a colour scanner which has become apparent following a number of complaints from customers, might be dealt with by a special group drawn from production, service engineering and hardware development.

It is apparent from this discussion of the three main types of relationship that integration of the organisation's activities may be achieved in many ways. The organisation chart tends to emphasise integration through the hierarchy, but the presence of a number of formal and informal groups with interlocking membership, and the influence of specialist advisers throughout the organisation, shows that the range of possible techniques for integration is much wider than might be suggested from a first glance at an organisation chart.

It can hardly be claimed that Small Print has a neat 'textbook' organisation chart. To an outsider there appear to be a number of anomalies. The relationships between the financial director and financial services, and the sales director and market research seem strangely ill-defined. The managing director appears to have a direct line responsibility for at least nine senior managers. This seems an excessively wide span of control. The personnel manager of the company has made a number of attempts to chart the organisation structure — only to find each chart superseded by new developments. Figure 4.1 is the most recent chart. He sees each individual's task in this technologically based company as amorphous, changing to accommodate each new situation, with little need for job description.

There may well be a relationship between the rapid rate of technical change in a research orientated company and the fluidity of its organisation structure. This relationship was explored by Burns and Stalker (1961) on the basis of research into the electronics industry in Britain in comparison with more traditional, less research-based industries. They suggest that two contrasting types of working organisations may be defined. In a 'mechanistic' system the management structure is well-defined and the members of the hierarchy are clear about their precise function in the organisation. Lines of communication and patterns of interaction tend to be vertical between superiors and subordinates, rather than horizontal between colleagues. This mechanistic type of organisation appears to be suitable in relatively stable conditions where products and markets are unlikely to change rapidly.

By contrast, in the 'organic' type of organisation there is more communication between colleagues, formal definition of responsibilities is more difficult and it is impossible to draw hard and fast dividing lines between functions. There are many occasions where the contribution of a member who may have a relatively low formal status, such as a junior research worker, has more 'authority' than that of a senior manager. In Mary Parker Follett's phrase, there emerges an 'authority of the situation' rather than an authority arising from status. 'Organic' organisation is most likely to be found in relatively unstable conditions where a business is subject to rapid technical, marketing and other changes and there is a constant regrouping of activities and responsibilities in response to these forces.

It is a moot point whether the present organisation of Small Print is a system of the 'organic' type which has arisen as a natural response to conditions of change, or is the result of failure to tie up the loose ends of a structure which has grown without much planning. Like many situations in the real world there may be some truth in both explanations.

Operations

Most of the decisions taken by managers are not concerned with such grand matters as setting long-term objectives, deciding strategy or designing an administrative structure, but with the company's day-to-day operations. In Chapter 2 we identified a number of primary systems in the enterprise — the technical, social, financial and information systems. During this discussion we encountered briefly some of the many operational decisions which the managers had to make in such fields as marketing, production, personnel and finance. In the next few chapters we shall look in more detail at some of these business functions and how operational decisions may be related to the long-term objectives of the business.

Before studying these functions separately it is essential to remember that a business organisation is a set of interrelated systems each of which must perform complex tasks. Some of these relationships may be illustrated by looking at a typical business decision: should a company install an expensive new machine in order to increase its production capacity? The proposal would need to be supported by information about the technical characteristics of the machine and estimated future cash flows, based on anticipated running costs for the machine, and an estimate of the additional revenue to be earned from sales of the product. For the majority of such project appraisals it should be possible to arrive at a decision given this information alone. On the other hand, if the machine is to replace existing workers, or alter the whole pattern of social groupings at the work place, an understanding of the proposal's social implications may be equally important. The decision now requires the balancing of marketing, technical, financial and social factors, and is clearly far more complex than a straightforward project appraisal.

Strategic, structural and operating decisions should be consistent with each other. How can Small Print's profit margins be improved? Is its organisational structure adequate? Why has the work force increased rapidly during a time of financial difficulty? Should the export sales force be reorganised? Is it possible to standardise component parts in the firm's products? As question follows question, it becomes more apparent that business success depends on the integration of many elements into a coherent policy.

CHAPTER 5

Marketing

The next four chapters will introduce the main business functions of production, marketing, finance, and personnel. What is the most logical starting point for this survey? The choice lies between production and marketing, and the decision we reach will depend on our view of business objectives. We may define the task of the business as the production of goods and services which must be sold in the best possible market. This is a production orientated view of business, carrying with it the implication that selling is ancillary to the main production task. The marketing approach starts with the customer. Whereas the production orientated firm tries to sell what it has made, the marketing orientated firm makes what it has found it can sell. All the activities of the business from product design and production to the final sale are planned with the needs of the customer in mind. As there is little doubt that a marketing orientation is more likely to be successful in the modern business environment, we shall therefore consider marketing before production.

Is Small Print a production or a market orientated business? The company has developed from a strong technological base and it is clear that its success in the past has been due to the ability to develop new products of advanced design. At the same time, the company has been able to anticipate the changing requirements of its customers and has successfully broken into some difficult export markets. Some evidence that marketing has taken a lower priority than production may be seen from figure 5.1. which is a section of the company's organisation chart (figure 4.1). The production and sales functions are coordinated by product group managers.

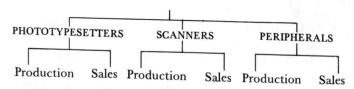

Figure 5.1

The organisation of these functions is therefore based on the three product groups rather than the markets which the company serves. This emphasis on product groups may not be satisfactory from a *marketing* point of view as many customers buy more than one product. In marketing terms we can define four market segments:

1 Newspapers
2 Trade typesetters
3 In-plant printers
4 Commercial printers

or we could define the market in geographical terms: home and various export territories.

The reader may wish to redraft this section of the organisation chart to give the company a stronger market orientation and to avoid the overlapping of sales effort which must occur at the moment. Figure 5.2 gives one suggestion.

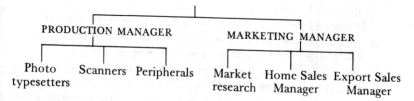

Figure 5.2

In the previous chapter we saw that there can be no single 'correct' way of organising a business. An organisation chart should meet the actual business needs of the company for which it is intended. In this case, the following points need to be considered:

(a) The new structure avoids the overlapping of sales effort which occurs at the moment.
(b) Market research is more closely integrated within the marketing function.
(c) Should there be further sub-divisions, e.g. home sales divided into market segments, export sales divided into groups of countries? Before coming to a conclusion it is important to take into account the number of sales-men and agents involved in each market (see page 60), a possible review of export sales policy (see page 62), and the need to limit the number of levels in the chain of command.

The Marketing Mix

A broad distinction is often drawn between marketing consumer goods and marketing industrial goods. It will be readily accepted that a marketing approach is essential in the motor car, cosmetics and processed food industries, but it is a common fallacy to believe that marketing is unimportant in industrial markets such as printing machinery. There are bound to be differences of approach between industrial marketing and marketing consumer products but certain general considerations apply to all marketing plans even though methods of implementation will vary with the type of product and customer.

It should be possible to define the marketing system of any business whether it is selling consumer or industrial goods or whether, like a bank or insurance company, it is selling services. The marketing system indicates the flows of information, cash, products and services between seller and buyer. It is important to remember that marketing is a two-way process. Not only does the seller communicate with customers to persuade them to buy, he receives market information from customers through the marketing information system. This feedback from the market is essential if business is to continue to provide the right product in the right place at the right time.

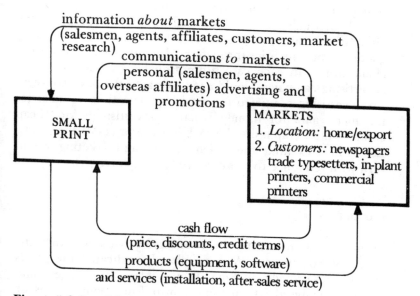

information *about* markets
(salesmen, agents, affiliates, customers, market research)

communications *to* markets
personal (salesmen, agents, overseas affiliates) advertising and promotions

SMALL PRINT

MARKETS
1. *Location:* home/export
2. *Customers:* newspapers trade typesetters, in-plant printers, commercial printers

cash flow
(price, discounts, credit terms)
products (equipment, software)
and services (installation, after-sales service)

Figure 5.3 Small Print: marketing system

Figure 5.3 gives the marketing system of Small Print in outline.

The marketing policy of a business is one aspect of its long-term strategy. If, for example, the company is aiming to double its turnover over the next three years it may reach this objective through adopting one or more of the following marketing strategies: market penetration, market development, product development or diversification. A detailed marketing plan will need to be drawn up to show how the company intends to reach its objectives over the period, setting yearly sales targets for each of the main product groups, market segments and geographical locations.

The implementation of these plans will depend on the decisions taken about the various elements of what is commonly called the 'marketing mix'. There are many different formulations of this concept but we shall adopt McCarthy's version which lists the 'four Ps' of marketing — Products, Place, Promotion and Price. A successful marketing policy means striking the right balance between these elements. The policy of market penetration, for instance, implies that goods of a high quality will be offered at an average price. An alternative strategy might be to sell medium or low quality goods at a bargain price through the discount houses or variety chain stores. In each case promotional activities such as an advertising campaign would need to match the basic strategy. An advertising campaign for market penetration would stress the high value for money whereas advertising for 'cheap goods' would emphasise the rock bottom prices of the goods. Let us now examine these elements of the marketing mix in turn with reference to our case study company.

Product

Production is the creation of goods and services to satisfy the needs of consumers. We have already indicated the goods and services provided by Small Print — its product range — and we have analysed its customers into four main groups or market segments. It is important to remember that the company is not merely selling a piece of equipment. Various services are usually included in a sales agreement including 'software' or computer programmes for use with the equipment, technical advice, installation and an after sales service. In the case of 'system' sales the service element is particularly important as the company will undertake to design a combination of equipment, peripherals and software to optimise the performance of the customer's entire typesetting department.

The concept of product cannot be separated from its quality. The various phototypesetters and colour scanners on the market differ from one another in their functions — speed, reliability, compatibility with other pieces of equipment and ease of servicing. In this type of industrial market it would clearly be unthinkable to produce low-quality equipment however low the price; no printer could risk recurrent breakdowns due to unreliable equipment. However, not all customers will require the same functions in a product and the company will need to decide whether to produce a sophisticated product for a specialised market, a simpler product for a wider market, or have a product range which tries to meet all possible requirements. It is clear that this product decision is closely related to pricing policy and indeed to other elements in the marketing mix.

The decision to manufacture a wide product range has also important implications for production planning. A company with a wide range of separate products, and variations of these products, will be unable to achieve a smooth production flow and undoubtedly will have a higher unit cost of production than a company able to use continuous production methods. There is, of course, scope for both types of policy, but a business needs to formulate its objectives with some precision if it is not going to get the worst of both worlds.

Even if it is decided to offer a large number of separate lines, the company should review the range periodically to prune items which are no longer profitable or which make an insignificant contribution to total turnover. This last point is closely associated with the idea of a product life cycle. Products will pass through a number of stages in their history until they eventually decline in the face of outside competition or a change in customer tastes. Figure 5.4 illustrates these phases for one product and also shows the importance of staggering the dates of new product launches to achieve a steady rate of growth for the whole company. Planned product development is essential if the company is to maintain an even growth rate over the years.

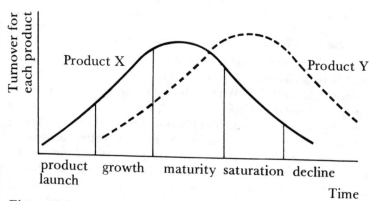

Figure 5.4 Life cycle for Product X

The concept of a product life cycle is clearly important in the case of Small Print. During its short history the company has introduced many new products and it is constantly seeking to improve existing products or launch new ones. It is therefore imperative for management to review the product mix frequently.

Promotion

The 'promotion' element of the marketing mix is concerned with communications from the company to the market. These may be personal communications from salesmen and agents or impersonal communications through advertising, publicity and sales promotions.

> Small Print engages in a variety of promotional activities. In trade advertising it matches the efforts of its competitors and places large advertisements in one or two journals a month. Every year a catalogue is produced giving full technical specifications for the standard product lines, and there are 'mail shots' to customers in the low price end of the market. Seminars for groups of customers are held in Small Print's extensive sales room where systems and units are demonstrated and problems discussed. In addition, each year the company is represented at two or three large trade exhibitions.
>
> The sales force consists of two groups: ten employees covering the UK, and an export sales force of four employees. Agents have been appointed in most of the company's export sales territories. Export sales representatives concentrate on 'systems' sales and on liaison with the overseas agents who tend to make sales at the 'lower' end of the market. Agents receive technical information from the salesmen and occasionally visit the London sales room for technical instructions. The ability of certain agents appears doubtful.

One of the most difficult problems in marketing management is to strike the right balance between different types of promotional activity. With a limited budget the marketing manager tries to achieve the best 'promotional mix' for the company. It is part of the 'conventional wisdom' of marketing that advertising is likely to be the most effective activity in marketing consumer goods, whereas personal selling will be more important in industrial marketing. However, the case shows that advertising has an important role to play in marketing industrial products. It is true that industrial goods are likely to be advertised through different media from consumer goods — trade journals rather than television, for example. The channel of communication must be appropriate for the market, reaching the maximum number of potential customers and gaining the optimum return for the promotional activity.

We have already a fairly clear idea of the audience for Small Print's marketing communications. The company hopes to meet the needs of the printing industry for machinery of various types but it is concentrating on the advanced technology segment of the market. This means that the company is more likely to be dealing with the more progressive firms in the printing industry, although as a particular type of equipment becomes more widely adopted in the industry its market may well widen to include more traditionally minded printers. Different types of customer may therefore be associated with different phases of the product life cycle. Promotion policies will clearly vary depending on whether the product is currently being sold mainly to 'early adopters' of a new product idea or to the 'early majority' of the market. There is little point in directing promotional activity to the 'late adopters' and 'laggards' who are likely to be sceptical of innovation. The reader may wish to assess the value of the personal and impersonal promotional activities carried out by the company in relation to these different types of customer.

The details given about the sales force and the overseas agents raise some doubts about the effectiveness of the personal selling function particularly in export markets. The question is whether the company has the best export strategy and is using the most efficient channels of distribution for its purposes, which leads us to the next element in the marketing mix.

Place

The 'place' element in the marketing mix includes such considerations as distribution channels, sales territories and methods of transport. Companies selling to a mass consumer market have to reach a number of difficult but related decisions about channels of distribution. Should production be carried out in one factory with distribution to a number of regional warehouses, or should the company set up separate factories serving different parts of the country? Should it distribute to wholesalers, retailers, direct to the public through mail order or a combination of these methods? If it is decided to distribute to retailers, which are the most appropriate outlets for the firm's products: department stores, chain stores, supermarkets, small shops, etc? Should the company have its own fleet of lorries or use outside transport facilities?

Small Print is not concerned with these issues and its distribution problems might seem relatively insignificant were it not for the importance of export trade to the company.

> The world market is apportioned between the four major companies of the Caxton group. Small Print has been assigned the following territories: the UK, the Middle East, the Soviet Union and Eastern Europe, Scandinavia, Australia, New Zealand and the whole of Africa. Each member of the group may sell within another's countries but only by transfer within the group. For instance, a sale by Small Print to a company in West Germany would be made through the French based company in the group; a sale by the parent US company to a firm in Israel would be made through Small Print.
>
> We have already seen that Small Print's export sales are handled by a small group of four representatives. This means that on average each export representative is responsible for twelve different countries. Good relations with the overseas agents is clearly important for this agreement to work effectively.
>
> Small Print usually undertakes responsibility for the installation of equipment, and in the case of systems sales the technical staff will make several visits to the customer's premises before the system is installed, during installation, and during the 'debugging' stage which could extend to a year after installation. Consequently, overseas customers often have closer links with the technical staff than with the overseas sales representatives and agents.

The main methods of overseas operation in order of increasing sophistication are:

1 sales made in the UK to foreign buyers and export houses
2 sales in foreign markets through agents appointed by the company
3 direct sales by the company's own representatives
4 setting up marketing/sales subsidiaries abroad

5   sales of 'know-how' and licensing agreements
6   manufacture abroad.

As a company increases its commitment to exporting it is likely to progress further down the above list of methods of operation. It therefore appears surprising that Small Print with 80% of its sales in the export market should rely so heavily on agents and have only four export sales representatives in the field. It is unlikely that the company would be able to consider such options as manufacturing abroad or the setting up of overseas sales subsidiaries, as these decisions would require financial commitments which are beyond its present capacity (see Chapter 9). It appears from the evidence that the company would be well-advised to increase its sales representation abroad and reduce the present reliance on agents. The agency system has often been criticised as a method of overseas selling. Good agents are difficult to find, they are unlikely to have sufficient technical knowledge of the exporter's product and they will be working for a number of principals including possibly direct competitors of the exporter. The agency system seems particularly inappropriate in the case of the advanced technological products of Small Print where direct contact between buyer and seller is desirable.

Many studies of exporting practice have pointed to the folly of 'exporting to 120 different countries'. The market sharing agreement between members of the Caxton group ensures that Small Print does not carry matters to such extremes but it does appear that the efforts of the existing sales force is being spread very thinly. It is difficult to see how the representatives can acquire that specialised knowledge of individual markets which is a prerequisite of success in exporting. Even if the sales force is increased it may be sound policy to concentrate on a selected number of markets.

Price

The importance of price as an element in the marketing mix will vary between products. In marketing expensive sports cars for instance, design, performance, product image and other non-price considerations are of prime importance and customers will be prepared to pay a high price for the right product, even though there are other cheaper models on the market. The market for standard family saloons is different. In February 1977 the Volkswagen Company issued an advertisement comparing their Polo model with Ford's Fiesta, pointing out that the two cars looked alike, had similar specifications (whilst claiming the Polo had the edge in some respects) but that the Fiesta was dearer by £80, less the price of seat belts. In this case price seems to be the crucial element in the marketing mix.

Apart from the basic price, the seller will also need to consider his policy on discounts and the credit terms he will offer. All these matters affect the pattern of cash flows received by the company as a result of the sales. In the case of industrial products such as expensive printing machinery, favourable credit terms could be more likely to persuade a customer to buy than a competitive basic price. This is particularly true of export markets where companies may often have the benefit of government schemes to assist the financing of export sales in capital goods industries.

There are two broad approaches to price fixing. One is to look at the demand for the firm's product and set a price in accordance with 'what the market will bear'. In its simplest form the marketing manager will look at the price of competing products and either fix a comparable price or a slightly lower price if his objective is market penetration. The alternative approach is to fix a price which it is assumed will

Table 5.1   Price estimate for Phototypesetter B39
              (full cost presentation)

	£
Direct materials	15,126
Direct labour	12,130
Overheads — 110% of direct labour	13,343
	40,599
Profit mark up — 20% of cost	8,120
	48,719

Proposed selling price: £48,750

cover costs and allow a margin for profit. 'Cost plus' pricing is the simplest form of this approach. An estimate for production costs is obtained by adding an allowance for manufacturing overheads to the direct material and labour costs of production. This cost is then inflated by an agreed profit margin (see table 5.1).

It will be apparent that any actual price fixing decisions should be a compromise between the two approaches. For instance, the market research department's assessment of the market for medium priced phototypesetters (see table 5.3) is based on the following information about the prices of Small Print's main competitors in this market:

Bembo	£41,550
Schoeffer	£43,600
Gutenberg	£45,850
Small Print (B39)	£48,750

An assessment of the quality and durability of the four products ranks them in exactly the reverse order. Is the 'cost plus' method of pricing producing a selling price which is higher than the market will stand or can Small Print rely on superior quality to compensate for this serious price disadvantage? Price cannot be isolated from the other elements of the marketing mix.

There are serious drawbacks to both the cost and the demand approaches to pricing if stated in their simplest form. In practice the concepts of 'cost' and 'demand' need further refinement if the business is to pursue a pricing policy which will come close to optimising profits. We shall then look at these variables in more detail.

Cost Considerations in Pricing

There is an important distinction to be made between the fixed and variable costs of a business. Certain costs such as raw materials and production labour will increase at the same rate as the firm's activity: these are classified as variable costs. Other costs such as rent and rates on the firm's premises will be fixed no matter what level of production is achieved. Actual cost behaviour is often rather more complex because some costs have both a fixed and a variable element: a telephone bill includes a fixed rental and a variable charge based on usage for example. It should, however, be possible at least in principle to separate the fixed and variable elements of all items of cost.

According to economic theory the relationship between total costs and output over the whole range of the firm's production capacity may be expressed as a curve whose general characteristics are given in figure 5.5. Fixed costs by

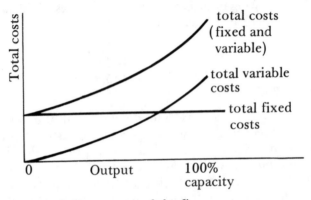

Figure 5.5 Cost curves of the firm

definition are constant for all levels of activity and therefore appear in the graph as a straight line parallel to the x-axis.

Variable costs will increase with production but it is assumed that as the firm passes beyond a certain level of output the 'law of diminishing returns' will begin to operate. This 'law' states that if variable factors (e.g. production labour) are added to the fixed factors of production (e.g. the factory buildings and plant) a point will be reached when returns per additional unit of variable input will begin to fall and variable costs of production per unit will begin to rise. If the production manager of a bakery continues to employ more and more workers, the point will eventually be reached where the number of loaves produced by each worker begins to fall and the labour cost per loaf begins to increase assuming that it is not possible in the short term to extend the bakery and buy additional plant. The variable cost curve will therefore begin to turn upwards as production approaches full capacity.

Although we must accept intuitively that some such point must be reached when production can only be achieved by working the fixed plant beyond its most efficient point, it is unusual for a firm to operate at these excessively high levels of output in practice. For practical purposes, therefore, the total cost function may be drawn as a straight line. If it is assumed for the moment that the selling price of the firm's products is constant for all levels of sales, the total revenue function may also be expressed as a straight line. These relationships may be expressed in a break-even chart which gives a simple visual presentation of the relationship between costs, profit and volume, showing clearly the level of output which must be reached before profits are made.

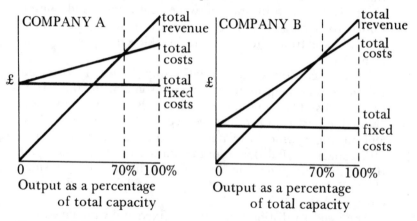

Figure 5.6 Break-even charts for two businesses

Figure 5.6 shows typical break-even charts for the two different kinds of businesses. In both cases, the break-even point is reached at 70% of total capacity. However, the relationship between fixed and variable costs differs between the two businesses which means that the rate at which profit is earned after break-even point is higher for company A than for company B. Company A would probably be in an industry requiring expensive fixed plant; chemicals or iron and steel, for example. Company B appears to require little fixed capital equipment but has high direct labour and materials costs — a shirt manufacturer, for instance.

The reader may wish to draft the break-even chart of Small Print given the following information based on the 1975 accounts:

Sales	£7.0m
Total variable costs	£5.0m
Total fixed costs	£1.5m
Net profit before tax	£0.5m

The production and sales directors agree that in 1975 the company was operating at about 85% of its total capacity. Assume that these figures give a fair indication of the general behaviour of the company's sales and costs and that these functions may be drawn as straight lines on the break-even chart. Is this relationship between sales, costs and volume similar to Company A in figure 5.6 or is it closer to Company B? Estimate from the chart the break-even capacity of the company.

This discussion of the relationship between costs and volume should help us to understand some of the limitations of the 'cost plus' method of pricing. Before we can speak about the cost of a product we need to know the exact level and output to which it relates. The unit cost of production at 50% capacity will differ from the unit cost at full capacity; in the case of Company A in figure 5.6 the difference is considerable. (Note: unit cost of production = total fixed and variable costs/output.)

The need to distinguish between fixed and variable costs is also important where a company needs to quote a special price in a competitive situation. Let us suppose that Small Print has spare production capacity which the directors now would like to use for manufacturing phototypesetters, to be sold in a new but highly competitive export market. What is the lowest price which the company can quote for a B39 phototypesetter for it to be worthwhile undertaking the business? The answer is that any price in excess of the variable costs of making the phototypesetter would yield a contribution to profits. Fixed costs can be ignored in reaching this decision because they will be incurred whether the company takes the business or rejects it. Unfortunately, the cost estimate for this product (table 5.1) does not present the relevant information for making this decision. We may assume that both direct materials and direct labour are variable costs but the figure for overheads will include part of the total fixed overheads which have been apportioned to this product in a somewhat arbitrary fashion. If we assume that £5,300 has been included as the fixed element in total overheads, the estimate could be redrafted as in table 5.2.

Table 5.2   Price estimate for Phototypesetter B39
             (marginal cost presentation)

	£
	£
Direct materials	15,126
Direct labour	12,130
Variable overheads	£8,043
	35,299

In these circumstances it is worth the company's while to quote any price above the marginal cost of £35,299. If the price quoted was £38,000 the company would achieve a contribution of £2,701 which it would not otherwise have earned. In the long term, prices must cover all the company's costs and provide a sufficient margin to finance necessary capital expansion, meet tax liabilities and pay an adequate dividend to shareholders. This should not prevent it from adopting a flexible pricing policy to deal with short-term tactical situations as they arise.

Demand Consideration in Pricing

The break-even charts shown in figure 5.6 represent sales revenue as a straight line drawn from the origin; a logical consequence of our assumption that selling prices remain constant for all levels of output. We must now relax that assumption because it is unusual for a firm to be faced with a fixed market price which it must take as given for all levels of output and equally unusual for a firm to be able to hold a price which it has fixed no matter what quantity of output it wishes to sell.

The relationship between price and quantity may be expressed in a demand curve, which shows the quantity which would be bought in a particular market at a given time assuming various hypothetical prices. There will be only one price ruling in the market at a time if we assume perfect knowledge between buyers and sellers, but it may be instructive to ask such a question as 'What would be the effect on the quantity of King Edward potatoes demanded today if the price were to rise by 5p a lb or to fall by 5p a lb?' to obtain an indication of the sensitivity of the market to changes in price. We would accept intuitively that a demand curve will curve downwards and to the right as in figure 5.7 because an increase in price will tend to discourage buyers whilst a reduction in price will encourage fresh buyers to enter the market.

Knowledge of demand conditions is essential if a company wishes to estimate the total revenue it would earn at various prices. Figure 5.8 shows the demand curves for two products P and Q.

The total revenue which may be earned from a given price can be found by multiplying price by the quantity which will be demanded at that price. For instance, if the firm sets a price of £10 for product P, it is estimated that 1,000 units of the product will be bought and so the total revenue at that price will be £10,000. If the firm now reduces the price to £5, the total revenue will increase to £20,000 because 4,000 units will now be bought. The case of product Q is different.

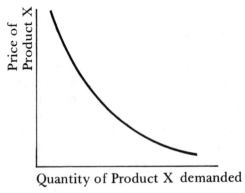

Quantity of Product X demanded

Figure 5.7 Demand curve of Product X

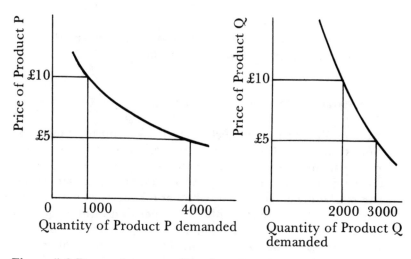

Figure 5.8 Demand curves of Product P and Product Q

If the price of Q is dropped from £10 to £5, the total revenue will fall from £20,000 to £15,000.

We say that the demand for product P is price elastic, or sensitive to price changes, and that the demand for product Q is inelastic or relatively unresponsive to changes in price.

> For Small Print demand conditions vary between products. Customers for the lower priced units (£5,000) tend to be more price sensitive than purchasers of 'systems'. Percentage profit margins are higher for systems as it is possible to add a higher percentage profit charge to the 'software' elements of a system.

It may not be possible to draw text book demand curves for these products but the marketing manager must be aware of the demand conditions of different products if he is to adopt a sound pricing policy. Such a policy would require a consideration of cost behaviour at different levels of output as well as an understanding of market conditions. In theory there will be a unique point where both cost and revenue factors are such that profits are maximised. In practice it is difficult to follow a pricing policy which ensures that this optimum level of output is reached, particularly in a multi-product firm. In any case it would be wrong to treat the pricing decision in isolation from the other elements of the marketing mix. The relationships between price, costs and volume are important but the pricing decisions must also be reconciled with decisions about product quality, methods of promotion and channels of distribution.

The Marketing Information System

We considered the general characteristics of business information systems in Chapter 2, with particular reference to a management accounting system. Similar principles will apply to the design of a marketing information system. Data about the marketing environment, whether it concerns relationships with customers, the strength of competition or more general social and economic influences, will be collected and processed to provide information as a guide for the planning, operation and control of marketing activities.

There are three main sources of information about these activities. The firm's accounting system provides basic information about orders, sales, and the state of debtors' accounts which can be used in marketing control systems. For instance, sales orders may be analysed by products, geographical markets, or salesmen and the results compared with sales targets. Secondly, the firm will have a market 'intelligence' system. As Small Print deals directly with the users of equipment, much of this information may be acquired first hand; salesmen in the field are in an excellent position to acquire information about customer reaction, the activity of competitors and market trends. It is important that this intelligence should be collated and assessed in a systematic manner. Finally, information about specific problems and opportunities will be acquired as a result of market research. The company may require a special study of the market for colour scanners or detailed information about a new export market. Although routine sales information derived from the accounting system and market intelligence obtained from salesmen and customers can provide useful, general information, the systematic analysis of particular markets needs to be undertaken by a specialist group of market researchers.

Table 5.3 Market research information (phototypesetters only)

(A) **Product competition** — ranking by relative strengths

Marketing ability	Design	Cost	Quality and durability	Manufacturing capacity

Phototypesetter B64 Medium price range (average £55,000) high speed

	Marketing ability	Design	Cost	Quality and durability	Manufacturing capacity
1	Gutenberg	Small Print	Gutenberg	Small Print	Gutenberg
2	Small Print	Gutenberg	Druck	Gutenberg	Druck
3	Faustus	Caxton	Small Print	Druck	Small Print
4	Druck	Faustus	Faustus	Faustus	Faustus
5	Caxton	Druck	Caxton	Caxton	Caxton

Phototypesetter B39 Medium price range (average £45,000) medium speed

	Marketing ability	Design	Cost	Quality and durability	Manufacturing capacity
1	Gutenberg	Gutenberg	Bembo	Small Print	Gutenberg
2	Small Print	Small Print	Schoeffer	Gutenberg	Schoeffer
3	Schoeffer	Schoeffer	Gutenberg	Schoeffer	Small Print
4	Bembo	Bembo	Small Print	Bembo	Bembo

(B) **Total world market sales (excluding USA)**

	High speed £m	Medium speed £m
74/75	3.5	11.07
77/78 est	4.75	15.25

(C) **Small Print market shares (%) 1974/5**

High speed	22%
Medium speed	31%

Source: Small Print; Market Research Dept.

This information about customers and markets forms the basis of the sales forecast. Other factors which would be taken into account when preparing the sales forecast include an assessment of the general state of the economy at home and in the company's main export markets, and the main business trends affecting customers such as the rising costs of book production or the growing importance of advertising revenue for newspapers.

The market research section is too small to spend much of its efforts on general economic forecasts, relying heavily on articles in the financial press, official statistics, surveys of foreign markets published by its bank and information from other outside agencies to assess the major national, international and industrial trends. It has been found that there is a time lag of between four months to nine months between the demand for printing products and the demand for printing machinery. Particular attention is given to such statistics as newspaper sales, books published and paper production. These 'leading indicators' will give advance warning of future trends in the demand for Small Print's products.

The company is engaged in industrial as distinct from consumer marketing and the market research work undertaken seems typical for this type of business. A company selling mass produced consumer goods would use different techniques of data collection and analysis. Small Print is able to obtain detailed information about many of its actual and potential customers. In the case of a product sold on a mass market, a breakfast cereal for example, it is only possible to collect data about a small proportion of the total consumers. In these circumstances the company (or market research agency employed by it) would need to take care that the data were collected from a truly representative sample of the total market. For example, the representation of different social classes in the sample should be proportional to their representation in the market as a whole. Having fixed an appropriate sample the information would be collected using such techniques as personal interview panel data or possibly questionnaires. An understanding of the statistical theory of sampling and skill in the arts of questionnaire design or interviewing are necessary to avoid the collection of biased data.

The Contribution of the Academic Disciplines to Marketing

Throughout this survey of marketing we have used material drawn from a number of academic disciplines. From our discussion of the Small Print case it would appear that the most important contribution is from economics. The marketing manager needs an understanding of the different types of market, the relationship between costs and volume in the firm and the general forces at work in the economy. The 'behavioural sciences' of psychology and sociology are also important sources for marketing studies particularly in the analysis of markets for consumer goods. Psychological concepts such as motivation, attitudes and perception, and social factors such as family circumstances and social class are clearly relevant when analysing consumer behaviour. The marketing manager needs to be able to assess the value of accounting reports both as a source of general marketing information and as a guide for taking price decisions. In obtaining marketing data, statistical sampling techniques may be used and quantitative methods of varying degrees of sophistication may be used to forecast market trends.

Marketing is therefore an interdisciplinary study, with each of the above subjects illuminating one or more aspects of the marketing problem. Although the manager needs an appreciation of the underlying disciplines of economics, sociology, psychology, statistics, etc., the contribution of these separate studies must be focussed on to the particular problems of marketing. The concept of the marketing mix emphasises the need to balance different considerations in reaching marketing decisions.

This problem is not peculiar to marketing. The interdisciplinary nature of business studies will be a constant theme in the following chapters on production, personnel and finance. The strengths and weaknesses of different approaches to the study of business will be discussed in the concluding chapter.

CHAPTER 6

Production

In Chapter 2 the technical system of Small Print was described in outline and it may be useful to recapitulate its main features:

1 The company has three groups of products: phototypesetters, colour scanners and typesetting peripherals. 'System' sales are made from combinations of phototypesetters, typesetting peripherals and 'software'.

2 Components are bought from outside suppliers and assembled into complex units built up from a number of sub-assemblies.

3 Any basic product may be modified to meet customers' requirements.

4 As the technology on which the products are based is changing rapidly, models are being continually modified. The average product life cycle is relatively short.

We shall now look more closely at this technical system in operation.

Purchases of component parts are based on the sales forecast. The design department prepares a complete list of parts required for each model and the sales forecast for each model is multiplied by the appropriate parts list to give the total parts requirement. The computer compares available stocks with the list of parts required and issues an order schedule. Bulk purchases are negotiated with suppliers and, in an attempt to minimise stock holding, deliveries from suppliers are then phased over time.

As production of complete items of equipment is in small batches or to individual special orders, it is clearly not possible to achieve the smooth flow of a mass production assembly line. One of the priorities for the supervisory staff is to ensure an even flow of completed sub-assemblies and products to the limited test facilities. Some of these facilities are often idle one day but have a backlog on the next day. While it may take only six hours to wire a circuit board, the same board could be on test for thirty-four hours. Other factors which frequently impose a limit on production are the availability of supervisory staff, skilled fitters and electronics inspectors and space for the storage of large components and sub-assemblies.

Productivity varies greatly, not only through shortage of certain parts, but by the occasional inclusion of defective parts that have passed the single goods inward inspector. Also there is an effect from 'learning' how to produce a new or modified product. The major cost reductions are made during the initial production of a newly developed product. The substitution of a printed circuit for a wired circuit has in one instance reduced the wiring time for a component from twenty-six hours to three hours. Often changes in parts are made after several units have been delivered to customers.

Production processes in manufacturing industry may be classified into four main groups:

1 *Job production.* Goods are manufactured in single units to customers' orders. Job production methods may be relatively simple as in bespoke tailoring, or more complex as in shipbuilding.

2 *Batch production.* Groups of similar items are manufactured together in batches but the numbers in each batch are not sufficiently large to obtain the benefits of continuous flow production.

3 *Flow production.* A single product or a relatively small range of products are manufactured as separate units in large numbers. Repetitive methods of production are used as in an automated plant (electric light bulbs) or an assembly line (motor cars).

4 *Process production.* This is the continuous production of commodities in bulk, e.g. oil refinery, brewery, sugar refinery. The raw materials usually flow through a number of processes during which chemical conversion takes place or impurities are removed.

Many actual production systems are combinations of these four types. Components may be manufactured in large batches and flow production methods used in the final assembly of the product. In the manufacture of such products as soap powders the early stages may be described as process production and the packaging of the final product as flow production. Some chemical products would be processed in batches if demand for the separate items in the range was too small or intermittent to justify continuous process production.

Small Print is another example of a 'combined' production system. Sub-assemblies are produced in batches of varying sizes. In the final stages, production is in small batches or single units to customers' special orders. It is often necessary to modify bought-out components and completed sub-assemblies to meet customer requirements. The production system is therefore a combination of job production with small and large batch production.

It is a particular feature of this type of complex assembly production involving advanced technology that it may take several months after a new model has been designed and put into production before all the 'teething troubles' are sorted out. Unit costs of production will decline as workers and supervisors become familiar with the job and improvements in the flow of work are introduced. Eventually a point is reached when further cost reduction becomes more difficult to achieve and the 'learning curve' flattens out (figure 6.1). Accurate estimates of product costs are difficult in industries of this type.

Production Planning and Control

J.K. Galbraith, in his book *The New Industrial State* (1967), argues that careful planning is becoming more necessary at both company and national levels as a direct result of the increasing complexity of modern technology. Modern production methods may require years of planning and the co-operation of large numbers of specialists. The introduction of a new motor car model may be taken as an example. Market research will give some indication of what the motoring public

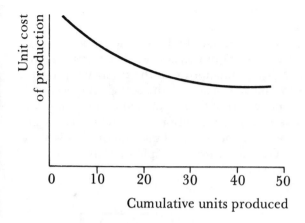

Figure 6.1 Learning curve for the introduction of a new product

wants and the designers will try to translate these customer requirements into a production model. Prototypes are tested and if satisfactory, production engineers will design the special purpose tools needed for mass production. Material requirements have to be planned in advance and where possible, the purchasing department will make long-term contracts for the supply of new materials and components. Labour requirements will be shown in a manpower plan, which may indicate the need for recruitment and training if shortages of particular skills are likely in the future. Marketing has to be planned from the initial market research to the advertising, selling and distribution of the completed model. Finance will need to be planned to cover the whole costs of the project from its inception to the eventual mass production of the new model.

Every important aspect of a company's activities will require planning and, as a corollary, a manager ought to know whether the plans which affect him are being implemented. Control is exercised when plans are compared with actual performance, and either action is taken to correct any variances from plan, or the plan is altered in the light of changed circumstances. It would, however, be wrong to consider planning and control as two separate functions; it is better to treat them as two aspects of a continuous process of management.

The concept of control may be best understood by taking the analogy of a simple room thermostat. The control system is planned to keep the temperature in the room at a predetermined level. A thermostat measures the actual temperature in the room and compares it with the planned temperature. The thermostat reacts to this information by switching the heater on if the temperature is below the limit and off if it is above the limit. Figure 6.2 shows the principle of a simple control system of this 'closed loop' type.

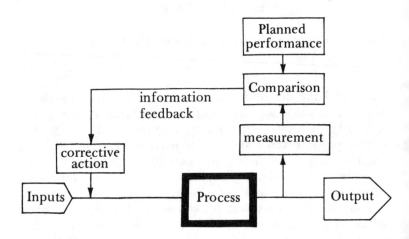

Figure 6.2 A closed loop control system

It is a relatively easy matter to apply the elements of the control process as shown in figure 6.2 to our simple example of the thermostat. In Chapter 8 we shall see how these principles are applied in management accounting systems through such techniques as budgetary control and standard costing. Control is a fundamental process of management and needs to be exercised throughout all functions and at all levels of the business. For instance, the idea of the marketing mix helps the marketing manager to control the balance between different marketing activities but the business would also need control systems regulating each of the separate elements in the mix; for instance, the personal selling function would be controlled by comparing salesmen's actual performance against their sales targets.

The case study describes the flow of products through Small Print from the supply of components to the despatch of finished equipment. We may also identify separate control systems for different aspects of the production process: stock control, production scheduling, quality control, etc. For each control system there is a 'feedback loop' in which actual performance is measured and compared with planned performance so that corrective action may be taken in the light of this information.

In the case of stock control, the company has to strike the right balance between keeping high and low stock levels. When the stocks are too low the factory runs the danger of production stoppages due to lack of components. There is some evidence in the case that production is sometimes disrupted for this reason as sub-assemblies are often started with missing parts. Conversely, the company might hold excessively high stocks of components. In this case capital which could be put to a more profitable use is tied up in stock which may deteriorate or become obsolete whilst occupying valuable storage space.

The objective of the company's inventory policy will be to avoid these twin dangers of overstocking and understocking. For each item of stock reliable information is needed about such matters as the holding and ordering costs of different quantities of stock, the risk of running out of stock at various levels and the expected time lag between placing an order with a supplier and the receipt of the goods in store. On the basis of this information it should be possible to determine the best level at which stock should be reordered and the most economic order quantity. Once these standards have been set, the operation of the control system should become a matter of routine. As soon as stocks fall below the minimum level an order is placed for the economic order quantity. The feedback loop is complete.

The quality control system attempts to maintain standards

of quality (i.e. physical specifications) and reliability (i.e. probability of continuing to function over a period of time). An electric light bulb, for instance, will be designed to meet certain specifications about the quality of materials, method of construction and safety standards. It will also have to meet standards of reliability expressed in terms of average hours of life of the bulb. In Small Print's production system, quality standards are tested at various inspection points during manufacture. Reliability is also tested in the final 'soak' process. Technical engineers carrying out after sales service of equipment also provide valuable information about quality and reliability. A complete quality control system covering all stages of production is clearly important as in some cases a faulty component will destroy an entire sub-assembly. Perhaps the company needs to employ more than one goods inward inspector.

Production control is a critical function for Small Print. There are two difficult problems to be solved: production scheduling and machine loading. Each batch of work has to be routed through the factory in the correct sequence. Components should be available when required, sub-assemblies should be finished on time and the final product completed in time to meet the promised delivery date. There are serious 'bottlenecks' at the inspection stages whilst batches wait to use the test facilities. A number of techniques have been developed to help solve these problems. Although it is outside the scope of this book to examine the operation of production control systems in any detail, we shall take a brief look at some of the techniques involved, mainly as examples of 'scientific' management and the application of mathematics to business problems.

Production Control and 'Scientific' Management

We have seen that the basic elements in any control system are a plan, measurement, comparison and a means for taking effective action. How effective is Small Print's *production control* system?

> For several years, the production departments had employed network analysis to plan and control, by monthly checks, the progress

of each product. As no work study schemes were employed at Small Print, the standards used for production control were estimates based on historical data. Without the staff to maintain the technique, it has fallen into disuse and has been abandoned.

Weekly meetings of the progress section of each division supplement the efforts of the foremen and supervisors in expediting jobs which are behind schedule. At the meetings the status of each product is established and progress monitored.

It appears that the weakness of this particular system is the failure to set adequate standards for production planning. An enormous amount of effort seems to be spent in 'chasing' products which have fallen behind schedule and very little time spent on preventing these delays from happening in the first place.

If the company wished to strengthen its production planning information, it would need to reintroduce the technique of network analysis. For each product a network chart would be prepared showing the logical sequence of the operations required in its manufacture.

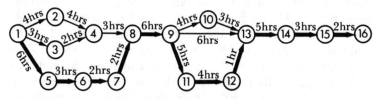

Figure 6.3 Network for a product

Figure 6.3 shows a simple network for the manufacture of a product. Each numbered circle represents an 'event': e.g. 10 means 'chassis assembly complete'. The arrows joining the events represent 'activities' which take a certain time, e.g. the time joining event 9 to event 10 means 'connect the motor assembly to the chassis'. Having set out the logical connections between the 16 events on the form of a network, the next step is to estimate times for each activity. These estimated times are shown in hours for all activities in the network. It is now possible to assess the total length of time required to complete the product and to check the actual progress of the work against these estimated times.

The form of the chart allows the production manager to concentrate his attention on the *critical path* or the path of activities which is likely to take longest to complete. For instance, between event 9 and 13 there are three paths, each of which must be completed before the work may progress to event 14. It will be seen from the network that the activities on these three paths take 7 hours, 6 hours and 10 hours respectively. At this stage in the production process the critical path follows the line of events 9, 11, 12, 13. The critical path for the whole network from event 1 to event 16 is shown by a bold line and the estimated time for completing the product is 39 hours. The manager must give priority to all activities lying on the critical path if the total job is to be completed on schedule.

The success of network analysis depends to a large extent on the accuracy of the estimates of activity times: Small Print's system failed because past experience was an unsatisfactory guide to current production times. Designs are constantly changing and even for relatively standard models production times may be reduced as a result of the 'learning curve' effect. Although it will be difficult to establish reliable times, some solution to the problem must be found if the production control system is to operate effectively. The company benefits from the application of scientific methods in the design of its products. If the methods of science can be used successfully to solve difficult technological problems, is it also possible to adopt a 'scientific' approach to management problems?

F.W. Taylor was the chief propagandist for the idea of 'scientific management' in the early years of the century. In the following passage he gives a pithy account of his aims and methods as applied to the task of finding the 'best way' to shovel iron ore and coal in the Bethlehem Steel Works.

> Probably the most important element in the science of shoveling is this: There must be some shovel load at which a first-class shoveler will do his biggest day's work. What is this load? . . . We would see a first-class shoveler go from shoveling rice coal with a load of 3½ pounds to the shovel to handling ore from the Massaba Range, with 38 pounds to the shovel. Now, is 3½ pounds the proper shovel load or 38 pounds the proper shovel load? They cannot both be right.

Under scientific management the answer to this question is not a matter of anyone's opinion; it is a question for accurate, careful, scientific investigation.

Under the old system you would call in a first-rate shoveler and say, 'See here, Pat, how much ought you to take on at one shovel load?' And if a couple of fellows agreed, you would say that's about the right load and let it go at that. But under scientific management absolutely every element in the work of every man in your establishment, sooner or later, becomes the subject of exact, precise, scientific investigation and knowledge to replace old, 'I believe so', and 'I guess so'. Every motion, every small fact becomes the subject of careful, scientific investigation. (Taylor 1947)

Taylor's approach foreshadows the development of a whole range of management techniques which claim to assist managers in the objective analysis of business problems. Work study which is one of the best known and most widely used of these techniques is the direct descendant of Taylor's investigation into 'the science of shoveling'. Work study embraces the techniques of methods study and work measurement and is employed 'to ensure the best possible use of human material resources in carrying out a specified activity' (ILO definition). Standardised procedures are recommended when applying work study techniques. Figure 6.4 shows the sequence of six stages which would be followed in methods study. Once the best method has been established the work will be measured 'to establish the time for a qualified worker to carry out a specified job at a definite level of performance' (BSI definition). It is often possible to measure jobs directly, usually with a stop watch. The production system at Small Print is such that it would be impossible to conduct direct time studies of all or even most of the jobs. On the other hand it should be possible to collect data about portions of jobs which have standard features and so build up 'synthetic' data for new jobs.

The principles of work study and similar techniques in the 'scientific management' tradition are clear and simple to express even though their practical application requires skill and training. Scientific management emphasises the importance of a commonsense, rational approach to business problems; the various techniques such as the 'six stages' in methods study amount to convenient practical procedures

1. *Select the work to be studied*
   Priority would be given to work on the more standard product for which there is a steady demand rather than special 'one off' jobs. Small Print might give particular attention to operations occurring at production 'bottlenecks' such as the inspection stages.

2. *Record the existing method*
   There are a number of standardized techniques for recording methods. Many are based on the idea of a process chart listing in sequence the elements of the task to be studied using conventional symbols for each element:

   ◯   operation

   ◁   transport

   ▽   permanent storage

   ◻   temporary delay or storage

   ☐   inspection

3. *Critically examine the existing method*
   This is done by asking a number of standard questions about various aspects of the existing method:

   purpose   —   why is the job done?
   method   —   how is it done?
   sequence —   when is it done?
   place   —   where is it done?
   person   —   who does it?

Figure 6.4

for achieving this aim. However, as business enterprises grew in size and complexity, more sophisticated techniques were evolved to solve some of the management problems which emerged in this type of organisation. The success of operational research in the Second World War in the solution of complex tactical problems such as the selection of optimum gun sites led to the belief that mathematics could be used more extensively in helping to solve complex management problems. This 'management science' approach can be taken wherever it is possible to express a management problem in the form of a mathematical model and apply the methods of operational research to find the optimum solution of the

The answer to these questions will suggest further questions to be asked. Why is the job done that way? Why does that person do it? This examination should suggest alternative methods for consideration. It may be possible to dispense with an operation entirely: delays and unnecessary transport are obvious candidates for elimination. Improvements in the design of tools or workshop layout may be required. Taylor found that the average load for shovelling heavy ore at the Bethlehem Steel Works was 38 pounds and with this load a man was able to handle about 25 tons a day. By progressively cutting off the shovel to reduce the load, it was found possible to increase the daily tonnage to well over 30 tons a day. The optimum position was reached when each man was handling 21½ pounds per shovel.

4. *Develop and define the improved method*

Once the new method has been suggested by the work study engineer it needs to be refined following discussion with other specialists such as the production manager and the design engineer.

5. *Install the improved method*

Consultation with the workers or their representative is necessary to ensure acceptance of the new method at the workplace. Relocation of plant and a training programme may also be required.

6. *Maintain the improved method*

Taylor found that workers often drifted back to their 'old, wrong and inefficient way of shovelling' if left to themselves.

Methods study — (existing job)

problem. Although the methods of 'management science' are more sophisticated than the techniques of 'scientific management', the basic philosophy is the same. It is the belief that management problems should be approached in the same way as problems in engineering; by the selection of the most appropriate method and the application of this method in an objective, rational manner to determine the 'best' solution of the problem.

To illustrate the basic approach of management science we shall take a highly simplified example of a production allocation problem which can be solved by using a *linear programming* model.

A chemical plant manufactures two products P and Q, both of which pass through two processes A and B. The company can sell as much of either product as it can manufacture and each product makes £100 contribution per ton to company profits. There are a number of physical contraints which limit the production which can be achieved in any one week. These are set out below:

	Process A (Total capacity 60 hrs per week) Hours per ton	*Process B* (Total capacity 30 hrs per week) Hours per ton
Product P	3	1
Product Q	2	3

How many tons of product P and Q should be produced to maximise contribution to profits for the company in any one week? If

x_1 = number of tons of P to be produced
x_2 = number of tons of Q to be produced

The problem is to maximise contribution (C) given the above constraints on production capacity.

This may be expressed algebraically as follows:

maximise $C = 100x_1 + 100x_2$

subject to the following constraints:

$3x_1 + 2x_2 \leqslant 60$ (production constraints Process A)
$x_1 + 3x_2 \leqslant 30$ (production constraints Process B)
$x_1, x_2 \geqslant 0$ (it is impossible to have negative outputs of P and Q)

It is possible to solve this problem graphically (figure 6.5). We first plot the production constraints for Process A and Process B as straight lines on the graph. Only combinations of x_1 and x_2 falling to the left of the constraint lines can satisfy the production constraints which we have been given. It will be apparent that only points in the shaded area satisfy *both* of these production constraints and the non-negative constraint (x_1, $x_2 \geqslant 0$). The shaded area is termed the *feasible region* because any combination of x_1 and x_2 falling in that area is a possible solution to the problem.

The final stage is to find out which of all these *feasible* solutions is the *optimum* solution. We need to imagine a series of parallel lines representing various combinations of sales of x_1 and x_2 which would result in the same contribution to profits. The dotted line $C1$ shows all combinations of sales which give a weekly contribution of £3,000. The contribution line for £2,500 per week ($C2$) is shown. The optimum solution will be that point in the shaded feasible region which just touches the contribution line which is furthest away from the origin. These conditions are satisfied when the contribution line for £2,142 ($C3$) touches the point M ($x_1 = 17.3$, $x_2 = 4.29$). The optimum for the week is therefore 17.13 tons of product P and 4.29 tons of product Q. This contribution of products will yield the highest possible contribution to company profits of £2,142 per week.

Because this problem is relatively simple, it can be illustrated and solved graphically. More complex methods of solution would, of course, be required in those cases which are more likely to be encountered in practice where a large number of products are manufactured subject to various production constraints. When it is possible to express the problem in the

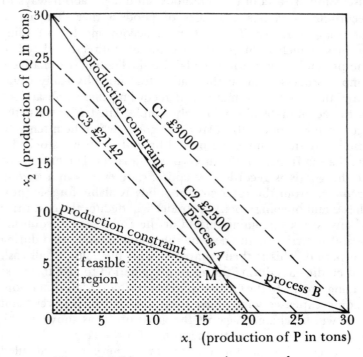

Figure 6.5 Linear programming example

form of a standard linear programming model a computer 'package' may be used to perform the routine calculations leading to the optimum solution.

The danger of treating one function of business in isolation from the others has already been mentioned. We shall conclude this chapter by considering the relationship between production systems and two other business systems: the financial system and the social system.

Production and the Financial System

In 1494 the monk Luca Paciola set out the basic techniques of double-entry book-keeping as part of a treatise on mathematics. This method of keeping accounts had been developed by the merchants of Northern Italy to record their trading activities and so it was hardly surprising that early discussion of accounting methods should be about ways of recording purchases and sales of goods rather than manufacturing activities. The system of accounting for a trading business which is in general use today is directly related to the principles set out in Paciola's book. Trading is a relatively simple process because the trader does not physically transform the goods; the method of recording these transactions in the accounts is also relatively simple. The trader starts the accounting period with a stock of goods which he intends to resell and throughout the period he adds to these stocks by purchasing from manufacturers or wholesalers. The movement of the goods is recorded by appropriate entries in a *trading account*. From the total cost of goods available for sale (purchases and opening stock) the trader will deduct the cost price of any stock remaining unsold at the end of the accounting period to arrive at the cost of the goods actually sold during the period. This is then compared with the value of all cash and credit sales during the accounting period to give the gross trading profit. In the *income statement* of a trader, other nontrading expenses which have been incurred such as rent and rates will be charged against the gross profit as shown in the trading account to give the net profit for the year.

More complex production systems require more detailed

accounting methods. Following the Industrial Revolution in the late eighteenth century and the growth of large scale manufacturing industry in the nineteenth and twentieth centuries, it became necessary to design accounting systems to reflect these new methods of production. A manufacturer needs to know the cost of his products in order to check that the selling price which he has fixed covers his costs and provides an adequate profit. The owners of the early small scale factories of the Industrial Revolution felt the need for this information. Josiah Wedgwood, the great entrepreneur in the pottery industry, admitted in 1766 that he had been 'puzzling his brain all the last week to find out proper data and methods of calculating the expenses of manufacture, sale and loss, etc., to be laid upon each article of manufacture, but without success'* In effect, Wedgwood was here describing the task of the modern cost accountant: to explain how total costs of materials, labour and overheads incurred by the business may be allocated and apportioned to the jobs, processes and other units produced. The cost accountant attempts to account for cost.

The techniques of cost accountancy are therefore related to the various methods of production which were discussed at the beginning of this chapter. In a job costing system for instance, items of cost will be charged to each separate order or job. Where production is in batches, each batch will be given a number and costs collected against that number. At Small Print, a technique known as multiple costing is used as this method is particularly appropriate for complex assembly production. Each sub-assembly is costed separately and as the work progresses, additional material costs and the labour and overhead costs of assembly are added so that the costs are 'snowballed' up until a total final assembly cost is obtained.

For a chemical works, brewery, oil refinery or other process plant, process costing is the most appropriate costing method. Figure 6.6 shows how the accounts in a process costing system are related to the flow of production. The reader should first examine the production flow chart in figure 6.6(a) and then see how the various inputs to Process B and outputs from

* Quoted in Pollard (1965), page 263.

(a) Production flow in a chemical works

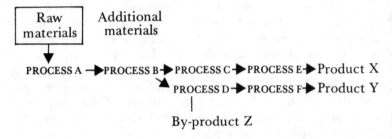

(b) Process account for process B only — July 1977

Inputs

	Production (tons)	Costs £
Transferred from Process A	100	24,000
Direct materials		5,000
Direct labour		4,000
Production overhead 300% of direct labour		12,000
	100	45,000

Outputs

	Production (tons)	Costs £
Transfer to Process C	30	15,000
Transfer to Process D	60	30,000
Normal wastage during the process	10	
	100	45,000

Figure 6.6

Process B are translated into financial terms in the process account (figure 6.6(b)). Whatever the practical accounting problems of these different costing methods the principle is simple: the cost accounts must express the reality of the production processes of a business in financial terms.

Production and the Social System

It has already been argued that quantitative management science may be seen as a development of the earlier idea of 'scientific management'. In fact, both F.W. Taylor and the modern operational researchers are part of a wider tradition which goes back at least as far as 1776 when Adam Smith published his classic book *An Inquiry into the Nature and Causes of the Wealth of Nations*. As the full title of the book implies, Smith set out to find ways in which scarce economic resources could be used most efficiently so as to increase total national wealth. One mechanism which he describes is the principle of the division of labour, and in a famous passage he explains how the output of workers in a pin factory is increased if each worker specialises on one particular operation. The logical consequence of Adam Smith's pin factory and Taylor's work at the Bethlehem Steel Works was Henry Ford's model 'T' assembly line. The task of building the first mass produced motor car was broken down into the smallest possible components. There were 7,882 separate jobs in the Ford factory, many requiring little or no skill. It seemed that Adam Smith's principle of the division of labour had been carried to its ultimate limit.

Increasing the division of labour so that each operative has a simple, unskilled task to perform may be an effective way of increasing labour productivity in mass production industries but the cost in human terms is more difficult to measure. Compared with a craft worker who may have considerable discretion about the way he carries out the job, the work of a typical assembly line operative is tedious, repetitive and rigidly controlled. Even the pace of work is outside the worker's discretion; he must keep up with the speed of the conveyor belt. Although the skilled craftsman may be able to see meaning and purpose in his work, there can be no intrinsic job satisfaction in repetitive assembly work; its only meaning and purpose is the pay packet at the end of the week.

In his early writings, Marx used the concept of *alienation* to describe this condition of the mass of industrial workers who neither owned the product of their labour nor controlled the methods of production. Many subsequent writers have drawn attention to the moral implications of the loss of freedom, initiative and creativity which is inherent in much modern factory work without necessarily coming to Marx's conclusion that this exploitation would only end when the workers themselves controlled the means of production following radical social change. Robert Blauner, in a book entitled *Alienation and Freedom* (1964), examined the position of workers in a number of different industries, printing craftsmen, textile workers, assembly line car workers and chemical plant operators. His main conclusion was that modern automated technology, in a chemical process plant for instance, gives the worker a degree of discretion and responsibility which is absent in flow production assembly work. Blauner was therefore optimistic about the spread of automation; it should increase the freedom and reduce the alienation of working people.

Moral issues apart, it may be doubted whether it makes *economic* sense to carry the principle of division of labour to the extreme case where the worker has no discretion about the way he will perform his job and the skill required is virtually non-existent. Such methods of production may be accompanied by disruptive 'side effects' such as an increase in the rate of labour turnover, absenteeism, strikes and even acts of sabotage. The increase in productivity gained from the introduction of 'scientific management' techniques could be offset at least in part by costs associated with falling morale and lack of job satisfaction. These costs may be difficult to quantify but they may be considerable, as certain companies in the car industry have found.

In recent years a number of companies, including Volvo, Saab, Bell Telephones and Philips have introduced programmes of 'job enlargement' or 'job enrichment' in an attempt to reverse this trend towards the excessive fragmentation of jobs and the removal of worker discretion. An assembly line worker may be trained to undertake minor repair work. A number of jobs may be grouped together so that workers are responsible for a complete unit rather than a small fragment of the work and have more freedom to schedule their own work. The value of job enrichment schemes and the scope for eliminating repetitive jobs through automation are a matter of debate; Blauner's optimism of 1964 is not shared by all present day writers on the subject. What is certain is that technical processes of production cannot be considered in isolation from the workers who operate the system. In any particular work situation, the technical characteristics of the task to be performed and the relationships with the group performing it should be seen as a complete 'socio-technical system' (Emery and Trist 1960).

CHAPTER 7

Personnel

There has been a considerable increase in the number of employees of Small Print in recent years: from a total of 60 employees in 1962 the figure has grown steadily to 763 in 1975 (table 2.1). The Administrative Manager found he was spending a large part of his time with the problems of labour recruitment and so in 1969 he appointed a personnel officer, George Smith. Apart from labour recruitment and training, the personnel section administers the welfare amenities of the company such as medical services, the sports club and the canteen. Personnel records are also kept for each employee. The personnel officer is responsible for ensuring that the company is meeting its various statutory obligations in respect of its workforce — under the Health and Safety at Work Act (1974), for instance.

As a result of this increase in size and the fact that Small Print is now a subsidiary of an international corporation, the character of the company has changed considerably since its early days. Small Print can no longer be described as a small family business but loyalty to the company is strong, particularly amongst the older workers. The Managing Director attaches great importance to employee motivation. In a recent issue of the company magazine he wrote, 'The obvious pride with which all employees greeted the news of our Queen's Award for Industry shows that adequately rewarded personnel will obtain job satisfaction in the broadest sense from company success'. Wages are at an average level for the locality and labour turnover and absenteeism are relatively low.

Very few of the workers at Small Print belong to a trade union. Some of the operatives belong to the Transport and General Workers Union (TGWU) and a small number of draughtsmen belong to the Association of Scientific, Technical and Managerial Staff (ASTMS) but attempts by this union to extend its membership to supervisors and scientific staff have so far proved unsuccessful.

Salaries are reviewed annually on an individual basis. Recommendations are made by the personnel officer following discussions with appropriate managers. Wage increases for operatives are given to keep pace with the rate of equivalent workers in the area. A payment by results system was introduced in 1972 but was abandoned in 1975 because of the absence of reliable work study data. There has been a certain amount of dissatisfaction amongst the skilled craftsmen who feel that their differentials have been eroded in recent years. A consultative committee has recently been set up to provide a medium for exchange of ideas between management and employees at all levels but rates of pay are outside its terms of reference.

As the above passage shows, there are a number of different types of issues affecting the people employed by the company: welfare, motivation, methods of payment, recruitment, training, industrial relations, manpower planning, etc. Some of these matters are dealt with by George Smith, the personnel manager, and his colleagues but it seems that they are primarily concerned with the 'mechanics' of personnel management: recruitment, the organisation of training programmes, ensuring compliance with legislation and the administration of training programmes. Personnel management, or the effective management of human resources is a wider subject than the detailed administration of the personnel department. It is the responsibility of all those who manage people in an organisation as well as personnel specialists.

This chapter develops some of the wider aspects of personnel policy which are implied by the case passage. The people of the business are first considered as an economic resource. Manpower requirements have to be planned in the same way that the company must budget for its other resource inputs such as materials and capital. It is obvious, however, that there are a number of important differences between people and other business resources. The remainder of the chapter develops this theme of the distinctive nature of human resources through a discussion of two topics: motivation to work and industrial relations.

The company may seek to obtain the maximum benefit from its expenditure on materials and its investment in capital equipment by the use of such techniques as stock control and capital appraisal by discounting future cash flows. Labour productivity may also be improved by the introduction of management techniques such as work study, by the installation of capital equipment and through training. Nevertheless it would be wrong to think of the worker as a mere bundle of skills. The manager who wishes to 'get the best out of the workers' is not only concerned with their technical competence. He must also consider such factors as motivation to work, attitudes to the goals of the organisation, and the appropriateness of different styles of leadership. The practice of these aspects of personnel management relies heavily on the behavioural sciences of psychology, sociology and social psychology.

Nor is labour a mere passive resource, malleable at the will of management. Different groups of employees may perceive events and policies in different ways and react accordingly. Management may talk about improving labour productivity by the introduction of a work study scheme: the workers on the shopfloor could see this as 'exploitation'. The behavioural scientist may seek to 'influence behaviour in ways that are consistent with the organisation's purposes' (Gellerman 1974): others might call this 'manipulation'. In any organisation there will be potential sources of conflict between different groups. Whether a particular dispute is caused by a failure of communication between management and workers or is the result of a genuine clash of interests may be a matter of debate. The subject of industrial relations is about the resolution or containment of industrial conflict both within the individual firm and in the wider business environment.

Manpower as a Resource

It is often said that people are the most important asset of a business. The word 'asset' is here used as a figure of speech because employees are not assets in the strict accounting sense; the skills of employees are merely hired to the company under a contract of employment. As the company does not have a property right in these skills they should not be valued as an asset in the balance sheet. Although this is still the accepted accounting view, there have recently been proposals for systems of accounting which would recognise the obvious fact that people in the organisation make a continuing contribution towards its success. The knowledge and skills of its employees are particularly important to a firm like Small Print, relying as it does on product innovation for its long-term success. Traditional balance sheets record values for fixed assets such as plant and machinery. Should statements also be prepared to show the value of a company's human assets?

Table 2.1 shows the present composition of the labour force of Small Print analysed into the main occupational groups. The company will need to compare these human resources with its future manpower requirements. Manpower plans should be closely linked to the overall strategic objectives of the company. Is the company expanding or contracting? Will product changes mean that a different balance of skills is required?

In some organisations there is a fairly simple method of calculating manpower needs. For instance, the number of teachers required in an educational institution will be directly related to the number of students enrolled on the various courses. The manpower requirements of a research-based, multi-product firm such as Small Print are much more difficult to establish; there is no simple formula for assessing the company's needs. An acute shortage in certain areas (export salesmen, for example) may be matched by an over-provision of other groups of employees such as research scientists. It might be difficult to give a precise figure for the company's needs in any one of these areas.

The company has expanded rapidly. Labour has been recruited as the need arose to develop new products and open up new markets. It is therefore inevitable that there should now be some 'slack' in the system and it is perhaps time for the company to look closely at its total manpower requirements and the way staff are deployed between departments. The recent deterioration in the company's financial position underlines the need for this review. At the same time, the company should estimate the size of the available workforce, making due allowance for losses through retirements and normal wastage. A comparison between future manpower requirements and this estimate of staff availability will reveal possible surpluses of manpower in some departments and deficiencies in others. The personnel manager will then be able to make his recommendations for staff recruitment, transfers between departments, retraining and possibly redundancies.

The mention of retraining should remind us that a manpower plan is concerned with the skills of the labour force as much as the total numbers required. Scientific and technological 'know-how' and marketing skills are particularly important in a business whose success depends on product innovation and the ability to work with a rapidly changing technology. As the following passage shows, these skills will be acquired through the educational system, partly through industrial training schemes and partly through work experience or 'sitting next to Nellie'.

> In 1973 the company appointed a training officer, but the movement of staff between jobs in response to product developments makes it difficult to plan a long-term training scheme for all workers. On the other hand, this continual transfer of personnel between jobs and the rapid obsolescence of many skills means that there is a constant need for retraining within the company. There is a limited provision of 'on the job' training in selected skills, and craft apprentices and technicians are sent on appropriate courses at the local technical college. Senior scientists and technologists often attend meetings and conferences to keep abreast of the latest developments. Recent difficulties experienced by the company in 'buying in' skilled technicians and craftsmen mean that it is reconsidering its training policy with a view to providing a more comprehensive programme of 'on-the-job' training. In general, there has never been any difficulty in recruiting well-qualified scientists and design engineers although the specialised nature of the company's work means that it is usually some time before a newly-recruited scientist or engineer is able to make a real contribution to the work of the research and development team.

To some extent a company is able to choose between a policy of training its workers internally or attracting workers who have been trained elsewhere by higher wages. In 1964 the Industrial Training Act was passed with the main object of improving the general quality of industrial training and Industrial Training Boards were set up under the Act to implement this policy.

Small Print comes within the scope of the Engineering Industry Training Board which is responsible for promoting the special training needs of all workers employed in the engineering industry whatever their occupation. The Act is just one example of a trend towards more government intervention in business matters in order to promote, regulate or control the activities of 'private' industry.

Many small or medium-sized businesses find that there are economies to be gained from increasing in size particularly as far as production, research and development, marketing and financial costs are concerned. A large company may have access to funds at a lower rate of interest than is available to a small firm, it may be able to organise its sales force more effectively and install advanced specialist machinery which the small firm could not afford. By contrast, so far as *human resources* are concerned, it would seem that 'small is beautiful'. Senior managers of small firms often know their workers personally so that communication is simple, quick and effective; a potential cause of industrial conflict is thereby removed. It is easier for staff in a small firm to exercise their initiative, unstifled by a bureaucratic organisation. The small firm is likely to be more flexible than a large firm in reacting to sudden changes in the business environment.

As Small Print grows in size it will probably find that problems in communication and human relations occur more frequently. At the moment, it appears that the company is passing through an awkward period of change. Small Print is no longer a small family business controlled by the founder but neither is it yet a large bureaucratic organisation. The company's organisation chart (figure 4.1) shows signs of this transitional status. If the directors wish to retain some of the human benefits of the small scale business whilst gaining some of the technical advantages of size, the organisation of the company needs to be carefully restructured. Business organisation, employee motivation and industrial relations are closely related topics.

Motivation

If asked why they work, most people would probably answer: 'For the money'. In one sense this is bound to be true because we all need some money for food, shelter and other basic needs. Some would interpret the statement more narrowly to mean that people work *mainly* for money, or even *only* for money. Whatever motives may influence his behaviour in other social roles, the worker is presumed to act exclusively as 'economic man' the moment he enters the factory gates. Systems of payments by results are based on this assumption that extra money is a powerful incentive to more effort. F.W. Taylor had no doubts about the importance of economic motivation. This is how he persuaded workers at the Bethlehem Steel Works to accept his ideas of more rational work methods:

> We want to pay you fellows double wages. We are going to ask you to do a lot of damn fool things, and when you are doing them there is going to be someone out alongside you all the time, a young chap with a piece of paper and a stopwatch and pencil, and all day long he will tell you to do these fool things . . . Now, we want to know whether you fellows want to go into that bargain or not, we will pay you double. If you don't, all right, you needn't take the job unless you want to . . . (Taylor 1947).

It is undoubtedly true that most people will work harder when paid according to what they produce rather than by time spent at work. There is, however, growing disillusionment with the actual operation of many payment by results schemes. Such systems are often unduly complicated, expensive to administer, easily 'fiddled' and may lead to friction between workers about the allocation of 'easy' and 'tight' jobs. In recent years a number of payment schemes such as measured day work and job evaluation have been developed in the hope of retaining some economic incentive for the employee whilst finding a more rational alternative to the 'piece-rate jungle'.

The assumption that motivation to work can best be achieved by direct monetary incentives has been attacked by social psychologists of the 'human relations' school. Between 1927 and 1932 an extensive programme of social research was carried out among small groups of workers at the Hawthorne Plant of the Western Electric Company. The results of the Hawthorne investigations are open to a number of different interpretations but many of the separate studies in the programme seemed to cast doubt on the theory that the worker is primarily motivated by economic interests. In particular, a wage incentive scheme which was introduced in the 'Bank Wiring Room' failed to have the desired effect of motivating the workers to increase production because the scheme was inconsistent with certain basic values which were informally recognised within the group. Workers producing more than what the group considered to be a reasonable level of output were branded as 'rate busters' whilst those who produced too little were labelled 'chiselers'. Elton Mayo (1949) believed that managers should recognise the force of this group feeling when considering worker motivation. The idea, which is implicit in the practice of 'scientific management', that human beings are mere productive resources, operating as isolated units and guided by economic motives alone was anathema to Mayo. He condemned it as the 'rabble hypothesis'.

Subsequent writers within this human relations tradition have been more prepared to recognise the importance of monetary incentives but would prefer to examine their role in a wider context. Maslow (1954) describes the following hierarchy of human needs:

Highest level of needs	Self-fulfilment, or self-actualisation
	Self-esteem
	Social needs (group acceptance)
	Safety needs (security)
Lowest level of needs	Physiological needs (hunger, thirst)

When physiological needs (the lowest level in the hierarchy) have been satisfied, they are no longer effective as motivators, but until they are satisfied all other needs will be irrelevant. A starving man does not worry unduly about self-fulfilment in an interesting and challenging job. As one need is satisfied, the next need in the hierarchy becomes the effective motivator. Maslow does not include pay specifically as a need in his hierarchy because he considered money as a *means* of satisfying various needs including the need for food, shelter, a secure and stable life and enhanced social status. Money is, however, more important in satisfying needs at the lower levels of the hierarchy. Maslow's concepts might be used to explain the 'Bank Wiring Room' results in the Hawthorne investigations. General wage rates in the group were sufficiently high to meet basic physiological and safety needs.

Applying Maslow's theory, it would follow that acceptance by the group has now become the critical need to be satisified. This conclusion is quite consistent with the strong informal group relationships which were observed by the Hawthorne investigators.

According to the managing director of Small Print, the effective level in Maslow's hierarchy is even higher for the employees of the company. Personnel are 'adequately rewarded' and so we m../ assume that their basic needs are satisfied. The references to employees deriving 'job satisfaction in the broadest sense from company success' and pride in the Queen's Award for Industry would indicate that 'self-esteem' is the effective level for many workers. Research workers may be realising their creative potential in the challenging work of designing and developing new or improved products. The achievement of this feeling of self-fulfilment through creative work implies that the highest level of human needs are satisfied.

F.Herzberg (1966) has provided an alternative explanation of the ways in which factors such as salary, achievement and working conditions affect the motivation to work. Herzberg and his associates asked two hundred engineers and accountants about the factors which improved or reduced their job satisfaction. Two groups of factors were identified in this study. The first group included company policy and administration, supervision, salary, interpersonal relations and working conditions. These factors created a favourable environment for motivation and prevented job dissatisfaction. They were therefore called 'hygiene factors' by analogy with the medical use of the term: the practice of sound hygiene measures prevents the spread of disease and creates a healthy environment. At the same time it was found that although inadequate salary or poor working conditions, etc. tended to create job dissatisfaction, good salary, good working conditions, etc. did not by themselves create job satisfaction.

Herzberg argued that the factors in his second group which included achievement, recognition, the work itself, responsibility and advancement, were the true motivators. When one or more of the factors in this group are present, employee satisfaction is promoted, but this only occurs when hygiene factors are also present. The common link between these 'motivators' is that they are all related to the intrinsic nature of the work; they are not merely elements of the circumstances surrounding the job. Satisfaction and dissatisfaction are not simple opposites; each is governed by its own group of factors, satisfaction by 'motivators' and dissatisfaction by 'hygiene' factors. To remove dissatisfaction is not the same as creating satisfaction.

There is clearly a strong similarity between Maslow's hierarchy of needs and Herzberg's classification of factors influencing the motivation to work. 'Hygiene' factors roughly correspond to Maslow's basic physical, safety and social needs whereas the higher growth needs in the hierarchy resemble Herzberg's 'motivators'. The importance of Herzberg's analysis is in its implication for personnel management practice. If his argument is correct, the provision of sports facilities, luncheon vouchers and other welfare services may improve the work environment but cannot act as positive motivators to work. Similarly, a high level of wages cannot be the panacea for all industrial problems. A payments by results scheme may lead to a higher level of output but by itself it will not create job satisfaction. This will only be achieved through the creation of possibilities for individual psychological growth. Herzberg considers that job enrichment schemes can make a significant contribution towards attaining this goal although, as we saw in the previous chapter, other writers feel that such schemes have a more limited role.

Maslow and Herzberg are two representatives of a 'school' of human relations theorists who stress the importance of social and psychological factors in motivation. The claim is made that a successful manager should cultivate an awareness of the factory or the office as a social organism and adopt a participative style of management. The obvious implication is that good human relations is good business.

This 'managerial' approach to the subject of human relations may be contrasted with the proposition that management *ought* to accept responsibility for the psychological well-being of employees whether this is good business or not. The business should create job satisfaction for its employees as well as goods and services for its customers. A full consideration of this view would take us far beyond the subject of motivation to work into a discussion of the proper objectives of business in an industrial society.

Industrial Relations

The managing director of Small Print holds the strong belief that all members of the business have a common interest in company success. The high level of morale amongst company employees seems to indicate a general acceptance of this view; there has certainly been no history of industrial unrest at Small Print. This picture of cooperation and good industrial relations contrasts sharply with the apparent state of affairs in certain other sections of industry in the UK where conflict between workers and management and even between different groups of workers seems to be widespread and deep-seated.

It is clearly dangerous to assume that all participants in a business whether they be skilled workers, unskilled workers, supervisors, general managers, or shareholders are bound together by a common view of their interests. Fox (1966) shows that it is often misleading to try to understand industrial relations problems in terms of what he calls a 'unitary' frame of reference which assumes that there is an underlying consensus between all participants. A manager who instinctively accepts a unitary view of the business system may be misled into believing that a problem in industrial relations can be dismissed as a 'failure of communication'. Even in a business enterprise which enjoys relative harmony in its industrial relations, each group may perceive its interest in a different light. Although management might wish to believe that 'we are all one big happy family' it may be more realistic to recognise the existence of separate interests which may sometimes be in conflict.

Small Print has only the most rudimentary industrial relations system. Few employees belong to a trade union and there is no collective bargaining at company level. The consultative committee is seen primarily as an exercise in communication between management and workers and its constitution reflects the prevailing unitary perspective.

A number of questions are raised by this apparently idyllic state of affairs. Morale seems to be high. The company still retains the ethos of a family business, there is a high proportion of professionally committed technologists and scientists and there seems to be a general pride in the technical achievements of the company. Does this optimistic picture of industrial relations in the company disguise tensions which exist below the surface and which have not yet found expression — the concern of the skilled workers about differentials, for instance? Has the absence of union organisation meant that the company has grown complacent about questions of industrial relations? Has the firm now grown to such a size that it would benefit from more formality in its industrial relations system, by the adoption of a grievance procedure, for example?

In the past there has not been much conflict within the company and therefore little need for machinery to resolve conflict. In recent years the company has expanded rapidly. Narrowing profit margins and financial difficulties mean that the company must now face a period of retrenchment with the possibility of redundancies and fewer opportunities for promotion. The company may have to deal with more serious personnel problems in the future than it has experienced in the past.

It may be instructive to compare the current position in Small Print with the industrial relations problems of the newspaper industry which is one of the company's most important markets. There is a sharp contrast between the highly structured industrial relations system in the printing industry and the apparent lack of system at Small Print. The following passage taken from a 'Guardian' article shows the operation of this system in one of the most difficult problems that the newspaper industry has to face — the effect of technical innovations such as phototypesetting by computer on employment prospects.

HOW TO SAVE £35 MILLIONS - AND LOSE 7,000 JOBS

Britain's national newspapers could be prepared for press at five times the current speed and with an overall annual saving of around £35 millions.

That theoretical option lies at the heart of the anguish and the aggro now nagging the industry. Soon, the unions will announce the results of their ballots on Programme for Action, the policy statement on print's computer revolution agreed by union leaders and the national paper publishers.

Even if Programme for Action and its outline of redundancy settlements for perhaps 7,000 workers is accepted by the Fleet Street voters - and that looks far from certain - there is still a long negotiating road ahead.

Yet many British provincial papers are well into the computer swim while Fleet Street has only tinkered on the brink. American papers, of course, have been heavily computerised for several years: the American Newspaper Publishers' Association estimate that by the end of 1977 every United States paper will be produced by computer-controlled photocomposition - the total is over 90 per cent already.

In contrast, only about half of the British press is photoset - and only two papers have crossed the demarcation lines, with journalists entering their reports directly into the computer, as happens in 70 per cent of American papers. There is broad agreement in the printing trade that Britain is nearly 18 months behind the rest of Western Europe and two to three years behind the US.

But before all this is categorised as a particularly lurid example of the British disease, there are other factors to ponder.

First, capital cost: the return on capital can be juicy indeed, but each unit of the ailing national press has to find between £2 millions and £3.5 millions for equipment. National newspapers inevitably need more complex systems than the local press.

The Royal Commission on the Press estimated in its interim report last year that the nationals as a whole could save £16 millions a year in wages for a total capital investment of £20 millions in the composing areas (where the typesetting and related work is done). But reorganisation and reduced manpower in other areas could raise the annual saving to around £35 millions. Redundancy payments would then increase the cost to between £50 millions and £55 millions.

. . . Above all, there is the human problem. Both managements and union leadership are clearly determined to avoid anything like the horrendous confrontations that have scarred the American newspaper industry, but a peaceful transition takes time. The problem is not solely economic: it is no small thing for a printer who has given a lifetime to a traditional craft to see his skills replaced by a sliver of silicone.

THE UNIONS HAVE THEIR DOUBTS

Reaction of the Fleet Street newspaper unions to Programme for Action has ranged so far from suspicion to outright hostility.

As soon as the document was published, the three main print unions, the NGA, NATSOPA, and SOGAT, held meetings of Fleet Street fathers of the chapel (the equivalent of shop stewards in other unions) to explain the proposals for improved pension and redundancy terms and a streamlined disputes procedure which it contained.

The National Graphical Association meeting was the most openly hostile to the plan. A vote was taken on a show of hands decisively rejecting Programme for Action.

At the National Society of Operative Printers, Graphical and Media Personnel meeting the document was also voted down on a show of hands, and in the next issue of the NATSOPA journal the union's general secretary, Mr Owen O'Brien, felt the need to justify Programme for Action and attack its critics.

The Society of Graphical and Allied Trades, whose leader Mr Bill Keys is chairman of the TUC Printing Industries Committee and the most enthusiastic moving force behind the plan, also held a meeting of its Fleet Street officials. Here there was no vote, and opposition seemed less virulent than at the other union sessions.

. . . Very few officials involved in the exercise are optimistic about the document's chances of success. The signs are that it will be rejected fairly overwhelmingly at least by NGA and NATSOPA members.

The most fundamental objection to the plan is that it will erode the autonomy of individual unions - through introducing a disputes procedure whereby, to some extent at least, other unions will sit in judgment on individual cases - and within those unions, will weaken the negotiating position of each house or chapel (union branch). There is also, of course, an underlying unwillingness to entertain seriously the idea of redundancy.

Mr O'Brien, in his defence of the plan in the NATSOPA journal, pointed out that those who opposed the document had put forward no better schemes of their own to cope with what he, together with other union leaders, regard as the inevitable technological advance.

The Guardian, 11 February 1977
Reporters: Peter Large and Rosemary Collins.

This brief extract illustrates a number of important points about the structure of industrial relations in the UK.

1. There is no single trade union to represent workers in the newspaper industry. This is in line with a tradition for skilled workers in British industry to be organised on a craft rather than an industrial basis. The three main print unions mentioned in the extract represent different groups of production workers in the industry. The NUJ is the largest union representing journalists. This fragmentation may lead to inter-union jealousies as the interests of one group of workers may often be in conflict with another. On the other hand, conflicts of

interest are not unknown within the membership of large amalgamated unions. For example, skilled toolroom workers might complain that the AEF, which is a large amalgamated union representing all groups of engineering workers, is not fighting with sufficient vigour to protect their differentials.

2. The case illustrates dramatically the effect of technological change on traditional skills and methods of working. The introduction of phototypesetting may be the economic salvation of the ailing newspaper industry, but in the words of the extract 'it is no small thing for a printer who has given a lifetime to a traditional craft to see his skills replaced by a sliver of silicone'. It is inevitable that some of the most difficult problems in industrial relations should arise out of rapid technological change.

3. The mixed reception given to the 'Programme for Action' document at the various chapel meetings shows that tensions can often arise between the leaders of a union and its membership. A trade union like a business enterprise needs to be organised for effective upward and downward communication. The office of the shop steward (or father of chapel in print unions) is particularly important as he is often the main link between members and the full-time officials of the union.

4. The case illustrates the importance of formal *procedures* in any industrial relations system. The disputes procedure recommended under the 'Programme for Action' was a means of resolving difficulties in the implementation of the plan with the minimum of recriminations. In many industries collective bargaining machinery has been set up to process wage claims and it is usual for these procedures to be exhausted before a union takes industrial action. Both trade unions and employers look askance at 'unofficial action' outside these procedures as this undermines the authority of the unions and leads to general industrial uncertainty.

5. The agreement between the Newspaper Proprietors

Association and the newspaper unions which was under discussion by members of the individual unions is not legally binding. Agreements between employers' associations and trade unions in the UK are not enforceable in the courts. This is in sharp contrast with the position in the United States where collective agreements are usually drafted as legally binding contracts. British trade unions have a traditional dislike of the courts as an arena for the settlement of industrial disputes and in general, trade union law recognises this position. If one of the print unions considered that the Newspaper Proprietors Association had broken a term in a collective agreement such as the 'Programme for Action', the union would be unable to take legal action but might take some form of industrial action such as a strike or a 'work to rule'.

We have seen that industrial relations systems are concerned with the resolution or containment of conflict. Topics of dispute may include rates of pay, hours of work, working conditions, union negotiating rights, job security, fringe benefits, pension schemes and provision for the effects of technological change. Disputes may be at national or plant level and a variety of procedures may be used in their settlement.

The poor industrial relations record of many industries, the car industry in particular, is widely regarded as a symptom of 'the British disease'. Why is there so much damaging conflict and what can be done about it? The alienation of workers in tedious, unskilled jobs and the problems of communication in the large firm have already been mentioned as possible contributory causes, but a full answer to these questions will depend on our view of the nature of industrial conflict. The 'unitary' perspective may be defined as the belief that 'industry is a harmony of cooperation which only fools or knaves choose to disrupt' (Fox 1966, page 5). In this view, all industrial conflict is an abberation which must be the result of a failure to understand the true goal of business. Whatever their sectional interests might be, it is better for all groups in the business to concentrate their efforts on increasing the size of the cake in the future rather than arguing about the division of the existing cake. The Marxist position lies at the opposite extreme. In this view, industrial conflict is inevitable because it is merely one symptom of the class struggle which is inherent in capitalist society. It will be necessary to change society as a whole before there can be a real change in industrial relations at factory level. Collective agreements and consultative machinery are mere palliatives which do not affect the cause of the disease. Between these two extreme positions lies the 'pluralist' view that a number of fairly equally balanced groups compete against each other for rewards in the labour market.

These different explanations of industrial conflict are associated with different recommendations for removing or at least containing this conflict. Job enrichment, better communications, training in industrial relations skills, and many other panaceas have been suggested. Growing demands for industrial democracy are in part a response to the feeling that workers would be more committed to the goal of the enterprise if they were able to participate in some way in the decision-making process.

There has been a growing tendency for the state to take a more active interest in the promotion of good industrial relations. The government will often intervene directly in a dispute which may have serious repercussions on the economy. In spite of the traditional reluctance of governments to interfere with the machinery of collective bargaining, there has recently been an increase in the amount of legislation and executive action in the field of industrial relations. In this chapter, we have introduced two examples of government intervention in business affairs: industrial training and industrial relations. Chapter 9 takes up this theme of the role of government and the law in modern industrial society.

CHAPTER 8

Finance

The contribution of men, materials, machinery and other business resources must be financed. In Chapter 2, we introduced the idea of a financial system representing the flows of money and money's worth between the organisation and its environment and within the organisation. As production systems become more complex, financial systems become more difficult to define and control. It is not therefore surprising that finance is often the critical function for many businesses and that accountancy is a rapidly growing profession.

In most companies, the accountant is responsible for the general operation and management of the finance function. His first task will be to install an accounting system to record financial flows in the business. The results of these flows will be reported at regular intervals to the owners of the business (shareholders in the case of a company). However, the accountant should be able to do more than merely record and report on past events, or act as steward for the business; his second task, that of financial planning and control, looks to the future rather than the past. In practice, it is useful to distinguish between two aspects of financial planning and control. Control accounting is a continuous process in which the actual performance of the business is regularly monitored against plans and budgets. Decision accounting is concerned with the provision of relevant information for particular decisions. We shall consider each of these aspects of finance.

Financial Reporting

The accountant is responsible for recording in detail the various economic flows through the business at the departmental, company and group levels. At the level of the individual company, an Income Statement, Balance Sheet and possibly a Cash Flow Statement will be prepared showing the profitability and position of the business. Economic flows through the various departments of a business are recorded through a costing system which will be designed to reflect its technical system (see Chapter 6).

For instance, the flow of materials from one process to another in a chemical works or a brewery will be recorded in a process costing system. Consolidated financial statements present financial information concerning the group as a whole without regard for the legal boundaries between parent company and its subsidiaries. In all these statements the accountant is applying the general principles and conventions of accounting practice to the various systems levels within the business enterprise. We shall concentrate our attention on financial reporting at the level of the individual company dealing with the two major reports: the income statement and the balance sheet.

Income Statements

The income statement reports on the profitability of the current operations of the business. It is closely related to the cash flow statement (page 28) but makes appropriate adjustment for the fact that many cash payments and receipts during an accounting period relate to a different accounting period. Small Print may sell a colour scanner to a customer in July 1975, but payment may not be received until after the financial year ends on 30 September 1975. The sale will still be recorded as a revenue item for the year ending 30 September 1975. The income statement summarises all revenue and expense transactions relating to an accounting period regardless of when the cash receipts or payments were made.

Income statements for Small Print Limited covering three

Table 8.1 Small Print: INCOME STATEMENTS to 30 Sept. 1975 (£'000)

	1973	1974	1975
SALES			
Home	764	1486	1420
Overseas	2920	4012	5544
	3684	5498	6964
COST OF GOODS SOLD			
Direct Materials	747	1387	1917
Direct Labour	1168	1790	2496
Manufacturing Overheads	447	611	741
	2362	3788	5154
Gross Profit	1322	1710	1810
OVERHEADS			
Marketing	298	480	510
Research & Development	278	448	460
Administrative	160	236	344
Depreciation (total)	70	92	140
	806	1256	1454
Net Operating Profit	516	454	356
Royalty Income (net)	30	60	160
Net Profit Before Tax	546	514	516

financial years are presented in table 8.1. It is apparent from
the most cursory examination of these figures that the profitability of the company is declining. There has been a small
drop in the reported net profit before tax over the three years
(a larger drop if royalty income is excluded) even before
making any allowance for the fall in value of money. In order
to stay in the same place the firm's reported profits should at
least keep pace with the rate of inflation. The need to present
accounting information in a form which takes account of the
changing value of money has been one of the most pressing
problems facing accountants in recent years.

Sales values have nearly doubled over the period but this
has not been reflected in an increase in profitability. In other
words, the company has been suffering from what might be
described as profitless growth. To examine this condition
more closely, we must look at the figures in relative rather than

Table 8.2 Small Print: INCOME STATEMENTS
(items shown as a percentage of total sales for that year)

	1973		1974		1975	
	%	%	%	%	%	%
Sales		100.0		100.0		100.0
Direct Materials	20.3		25.3		27.6	
Direct Labour	31.7		32.6		35.8	
Manufacturing Overhead	12.1		11.1		10.6	
Cost of Goods Sold		64.1		69.0		74.0
Gross Profit		35.9		31.0		26.0
Non Manufacturing Overheads	21.9		22.8		20.9	
Royalty Income	0.8	21.1	1.1	21.7	2.3	18.6
Net Profit Before Tax		14.8		9.3		7.4

absolute terms. Table 8.2 expresses the main elements of the income statement as percentages of total sales. As a percentage of sales net profit in 1975 is exactly half the 1973 level. Manufacturing and non-manufacturing overhead is taking a slightly lower percentage although we must remember that this is a significant increase in absolute terms. This is a rather surprising result. As there is a fairly large fixed cost element in overhead expenses, it might be reasonable to assume that a doubling of sales during the period would lead to a marked reduction in overhead costs expressed as a percentage of sales. An examination of the full income statement shows that although administrative and manufacturing overheads have continued to rise there has been some attempt to restrain the growth in marketing and research costs during 1975.

The main problem seems to be with the variable costs: direct materials and labour. Materials in particular have risen from 20.3% of sales to 27.6% of sales. It is the gross profit margins of the company that are being eroded. We are driven to the conclusion that the company's prices are not keeping pace with the increased cost of materials and labour or that it is deliberately cutting its margins, possibly to break into difficult new export markets.

Table 8.3 Small Print: Balance Sheets* £'000s

	1973	1974	1975
FIXED ASSETS			
Leasehold Premises (net)	60	50	40
Plant and Equipment (net)	242	361	480
	302	411	520
CURRENT ASSETS			
Stock (net)	430	843	1002
Debtors (net) —			
Home Customers	94	318	909
Overseas Affiliates	641	1047	1817
Bank and Cash	48	12	80
Total Current Assets	1213	2220	3808
CURRENT LIABILITIES			
Taxation owing	(237)	(294)	(312)
Creditors	(271)	(655)	(1440)
Loans	(24)	(430)	(987)
Total Current Liabilities	(532)	(1379)	(2739)
Net Current Assets (Working Capital)	681	841	1069
Total Net Assets	983	1252	1589
FINANCED BY:			
Caxton Equity	40	40	40
Retained Earnings	943	1212	1549
Total Caxton Equity	983	1252	1589

* The balance sheets show the position at 30 September for each year.

Balance Sheet

The effect of this period of rapid but profitless growth may be seen in the balance sheets of the company at the end of the three financial years (table 8.3).

It is now possible to give an additional measure of the profitability of the company: when the net profit is shown as a percentage of total fixed and current assets we see a sharp decline from 36.0% in 1973 to 11.9% in 1975. This is a measure of how efficiently the business is using its assets. A return of 11.9% on capital employed in a risky business does not seem very high, particularly when this rate is compared with a yield before tax on gilt edged securities of 14.7% in 1975.*

A further point emerges from figure 8.1 which shows the balance sheet information for 1973 and 1975 in the form of bar charts. In this case there has been a rapid rise in both current assets and current liabilities and the proportion of total assets attributable to the company (or its parent company, Caxton Ltd) has declined. The business has become more vulnerable to outside pressures.

As the proportion of liabilities to outsiders grows, the risk increases that the company will be unable to meet its commitments without recourse to assistance from Caxton.

The ratio of current liabilities to current assets is another important financial index. It gives an indication of the company's 'working capital' — the extent to which current assets (cash, debtors, stock) are available to meet the operational needs of the business rather than the pressing demands of creditors. The ratio has dropped from 1:2.28 in 1973 to 1:1.39 in 1975. A closer examination of the position of accounts receivable (debtors) and accounts payable (creditors) is a further illustration of the company's worsening financial position.

Debtors

Photosetting equipment is sold on deferred terms, the usual cash with order being 20% of the sales price. Keyboards are sold on a normal 30-60 day account. Over the three years covered by the accounts there has been a lengthening of the average period of credit allowed to customers, viz:

3rd quarter 1972	63 days
3rd quarter 1973	103 days
3rd quarter 1974	126 days

* Yield on 2½% Consols: average of working days during 1975.

There are three main reasons why creditors have been taking longer on average to settle their accounts:

(1) The general tightness of money in the UK in 1974/5.
(2) Delays in payment of accounts due to technical problems with the equipment or related 'software'.
(3) Difficulties in obtaining prompt payment from certain countries in the Middle East.

Creditors

The cash shortage in the UK during this period also meant that suppliers were anxious to secure prompt payment of their accounts. However, an examination of the accounts shows there has been an *increase* of £785,000 in creditors between 1974 and 1975. The period of credit taken by the company has increased substantially and this has imposed

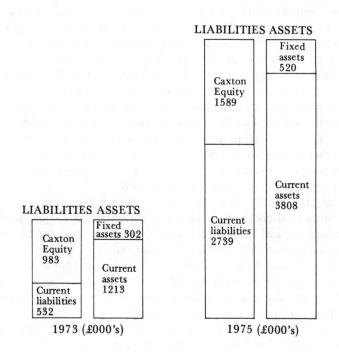

Figure 8.1 Small Print: balance sheets 1973 and 1975

a severe strain on relations with suppliers, many of whom were threatening to stop further deliveries unless payment was made.

There is therefore every indication that the company is 'overtrading' or expanding its business beyond its available resources of working capital.

Planning and Control

Throughout our discussion of the marketing, production, and personnel functions, we have constantly been reminded of the importance of planning in modern business. Marketing plans based on thorough research into market requirements, planning of material requirements, production scheduling and manpower plans have all been introduced and related to the overriding need for a long-term strategic plan.

The management accountant makes an essential contribution to this process. He is of course responsible for advising the directors on the planning of company finance, for safeguarding the long-term capital needs of the company and avoiding the sort of liquidity problem that will be facing Small Print unless it curbs its tendency to overtrade. He is also responsible for assessing the financial implication of the strategic and operating plans of the business. Budgetary control is the attempt to coordinate all the operations of the business; marketing, production and other plans are expressed in financial terms and all these activities are integrated into a comprehensive budgetary control system.

Budgets are not, therefore, mere accounting exercises but the means whereby the company's policies are expressed, coordinated and controlled. They should be related to the organisational structure of the company so that each manager's budget reflects his responsibilities. It is essential that managers cooperate in the preparation of their budgets and agree that they set attainable goals. The accountant is clearly dependent on the expertise of marketing, production, personnel and other specialist managers for the technical data on which the budgets must be based. Equally important is the need for managers to accept that they are participating in a worthwhile exercise and that the budgets are seen to be realistic by them. This coordination is often achieved through a budget committee consisting of senior managers working closely with the management accountant.

The two main purposes of budgetary control are profit planning, through the coordination of the various operating budgets, and resource budgeting. Although it is convenient to examine each group of budgets separately, it should be remembered that both form part of a coordinated system.

Operating Budgets

The preparation of the separate budgets in the system should follow a logical sequence. The starting point is determined by the major factor constraining future growth of the company. In the case of Small Print this factor has traditionally been sales volume, but when preparing the sales budget for the accounting year ending 30 September 1976 the budget committee was conscious that profit margins would need to be increased, even though an increase in prices would reduce sales volume. A detailed examination of all markets, home and abroad, was undertaken to ensure that the pricing policy adopted would maximise total revenue from sales.

Having set the sales budget the committee will then consider the other main budgets. Figure 8.2 shows some of the relationships within the budgetary control system and examples of policy decisions which must be taken into account when setting individual budgets. Information from strategic, marketing, purchasing, production and manpower plans will be incorporated at the appropriate stage. As the committee proceeds it will discover 'bottlenecks' which will force it to reconsider plans which had previously been agreed. For instance, the production budget for colour scanners may imply a labour force with certain skills well above current manpower forecasts. This means that production and sales plans would have to be scaled down to meet this newly discovered 'limiting factor'. If the final result is to be realistic, all inconsistencies between budgets will have to be removed.

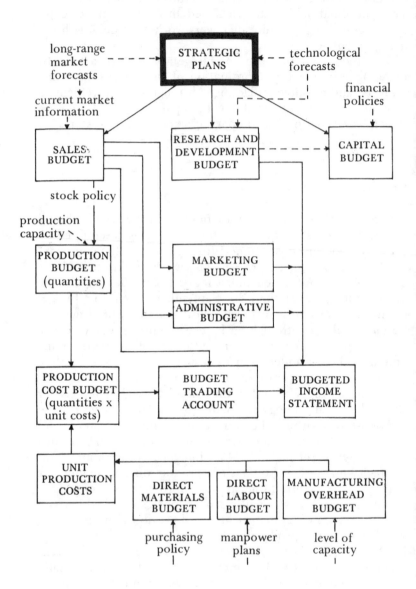

Figure 8.2 Small Print: budgets for profit planning

Policy decisions which will affect budget levels for the year ending
September 1976:

1. **Stock Policy.** It has been decided to run down stocks to about
   their value at the end of 1974 (e.g. a reduction of £150,000 over
   the year) in an attempt to improve the working capital position.
2. **Marketing Budget, Administrative Budgets.** These will be held at
   the 1975 level in spite of a planned increase of 12% in sales
   revenue. Various economies and a redeployment of sales staff
   have been recommended.
3. **Research and Development Budget.** No major new projects will
   be started. The main development effort will be in the improvement of existing products to obtain a higher degree of technical
   compatibility.

Note: Sales and Production budgets will be analysed into the main
      product groups. Each manager will be presented with a budget
      relating to all expenditure under his control.

Resource Budgets

In addition to planning for profit the budgetary control
system will also plan to ensure that the resources of materials,
labour, capital and cash are available when required. The
materials and labour budgets have already been introduced.
Capital budgets will be prepared for several years in advance
because investment in new projects will need to be related to
the long-term strategic plan. Each individual capital project
will be the subject of a separate appraisal (see page 132 for an
examination of a research and development project).

Many businesses have failed not because they were necessarily unprofitable but because they ran short of working
capital. We have already seen, through an examination of the
cash flow statement (page 28) and balance sheet (page 117),
that Small Print is facing a serious cash crisis. The preparation
of the cash budget for the following year is therefore a matter
of considerable importance (figure 8.3). Given the average
periods of credit given and received, cash payments to
creditors and cash receipts from debtors may be deduced. If
the cash budget is prepared on a month by month basis,
possible shortages of cash at various times of the year will be
anticipated. If the shortage is merely temporary, the accountant will probably arrange a bank overdraft. If the shortage is

more permanent, longer-term finance from the parent company may be required.

It is more probable that this exercise of preparing the cash budget will bring home to the managers of Small Print the serious danger of overtrading that they are now facing. They may then consider it prudent to cut back on the planned rate

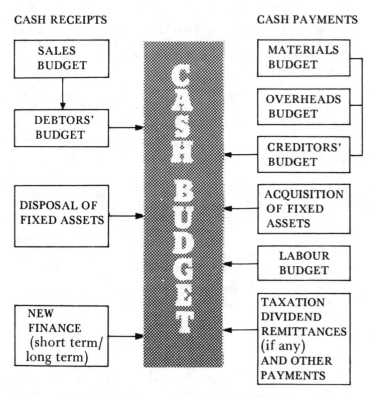

Figure 8.3 Elements of a typical cash budget

of expansion for the financial year ending September 1976. It may not be possible to obtain credit for the additional materials which would be required if the company is to meet the budgeted 12% increase in sales revenue. Cash has become the new limiting factor and all other plans must be adjusted accordingly.

In our discussion of production systems (page 80) we saw that *control* involves the comparison of actual performance with an agreed standard and the feedback of information to management about any significant deviations from plan, so that effective remedial action may be taken. Accounting control systems operate on a similar principle. Actual expenditure by a particular department will be compared with the agreed budget for that department and particular attention paid to overspending. A particular feature of this type of management accounting is that it directs the attention of managers to the exceptional cases; there is usually no need to worry unduly when a department is operating according to plan.

In standard costing systems, which are designed to control the costs of products rather than departments, an attempt is made to analyse the cause of any 'variances' from standard. Separate materials, labour and overhead variances will be prepared and each of these analysed to give a more specific guide to possible management action. Thus, the total materials variance will be analysed into a price variance and a usage variance.

Small Print has installed a standard costing system to control material, labour and manufacturing overhead costs. In one particular month an unfavourable materials variance is reported, which shows that in the colour scanner production the usage of materials is 30% higher than the predetermined standard. An investigation reveals the following:

(a) The adverse materials usage variance is caused by a high scrap rate.
(b) Most of the scrap is caused by untrained labour employed in the department.
(c) The heavy demand at peak times makes it necessary to use untrained labour at these times to meet urgent delivery dates.

This analysis of the situation by variance analysis helps management to define the problem, although as with many business problems there is no self-evident solution. If the operative 'cause' of the scrap is untrained labour, the solution might be an improved training programme. If the uneven production flow is seen as the cause, the answer might lie in improved production scheduling, or in the launching of a new product designed to balance out the peak demand. It is also possible that the 'problem' is caused because the inspection standards are unnecessarily high, and that the production has been wrongly classified as 'scrap'.

A management accounting report is therefore more than the end product of a lengthy process of recording, classifying and analysing financial data. In addition to producing information, the accountant must be an effective communicator of that information. Managers must be able to understand the meaning of the various reports which they receive and they should have confidence in their value to them as a basis for action. It is rather naive to assume that when the accountant reports on unfavourable variances the manager concerned will immediately try to put things right. As we saw in the previous chapter, motivation is a complex subject. Too often accountants have concentrated on the technical aspects of setting budgets and calculating variances rather than looking at the way in which the variance information is actually used by managers.

In an early study of the impact of budgets on people Argyris (1952) found that supervisors often think of budgets as devices introduced by management to restrict their freedom of action unreasonably. He claimed that in the long run such authoritarian budgetary practices are counter-productive. Any gains resulting from tighter financial control will be offset by a fall in morale and a reduced willingness to work towards corporate goals. Budgets are not simply exercises in financial arithmetic; they relate to people. Genuine cooperation with the managers in setting their targets is essential if budgets are to be an effective management control.

Decision Accounting

The financial accounting system produces income statements, cash flow statements and balance sheets for the company as a whole. Cost accounting is concerned with the preparation of information about the detailed costs of the firm's products, processes and departments, and reporting this information to management at regular intervals. In the case of an historical cost finding system the cost accountant records, classifies, and reports actual costs. Standard costing and budgetary control systems incorporate cost standards as a basis for the planning and control of future business activities. In all these cases, the accounting system produces regular information for managers and also, in the case of the financial accounting system, for shareholders, investors and the public at large.

A business decision is a unique event whether it is a decision to install a new machine, fix a selling price, lease or buy a piece of equipment, make or buy out a component part or drop an existing product. When making a decision, managers will need to select from the mass of available data whatever information is appropriate for that decision. A decision to launch a new product will depend on marketing, technical and financial information. It is necessary to quantify all the relevant costs and benefits for a complete evaluation of the proposal and this information will be produced specially for use in making that particular decision. Routine accounting reports will be of limited value for this purpose.

For the remainder of this chapter we shall outline the main considerations that must be borne in mind when collecting and processing data for use as a guide to decision making whether it be a short-term tactical decision or the evaluation of a long-term capital project. It is not possible to describe the techniques of decision accounting in any detail; our main concern is to describe the principles behind the various techniques.

When evaluating alternative projects it is important to make sure that only *relevant* costs and benefits are considered. Let us assume that the production manager has to decide whether or not to scrap an existing machine and replace it with a new one costing £10,000. The old machine cost £5,000 five years ago, and, as it is being depreciated at £500 per annum, its 'written down' value is now £2,500. The manager must decide whether the estimated future benefits from installing the new machine will justify the outlay of £10,000. In reaching his decision he should not be influenced by the original cost of the old machine (£5,000). This is a committed or 'sunk' cost and nothing to be decided now will alter that fact. The annual depreciation charge should also be ignored because depreciation is essentially an accounting device to apportion the original cost of the machine over its estimated life. On the other hand, the future running costs of the old machine will need to be included in the comparison. There is no commitment to these future running costs; they may be avoided if the old machine is scrapped and the new machine installed. Any scrap value of old machines would also have to be included — future costs are relevant but 'sunk' costs must be ignored. When making these comparisons between alternative proposals, costs which are common to all the proposals may be ignored. It is only *differences* in cost between proposals which are relevant.

Let us now suppose the production manager wants to stop production of a particular circuit board because of the difficulties of scheduling the work. He suggests that, in future, circuit boards could be purchased from an outside supplier.

An investigation by the cost accountant reveals the following:

Circuit Board B 178		*Current Costs*
	£	£
Materials		9.00
Labour:		
(1) Assembly 6hrs @ £1.75 per hr	10.50	
(2) Test 2hrs @ £2.50 per hr	5.00	
		15.50
Variable manufacturing overhead:		
33 $\frac{1}{3}$% of labour costs		5.17
Total variable costs		29.67
Fixed manufacturing overhead:		
20% of labour costs		3.10
Total manufacturing cost		32.77

The purchasing manager has received a quotation of £30 per circuit board from a reputable supplier provided a minimum order of 500 will be placed, deliveries to be spread over a nine-month period. Selling and administrative overheads are irrelevant to the decision as these will have to be incurred eventually whether the part is made at Small Print or bought from the supplier. The fixed manufacturing overhead is also irrelevant as these costs (factory rent, for example) will be incurred whether the company makes the circuit board or not.

The total variable cost of £29.67 is the relevant cost and so it appears from this evidence that it is marginally less profitable to buy the component from the outside supplier. A closer examination of the costing information provided shows that the figure for variable overheads is an estimate based on the existing method of production. If the policy of buying out leads to a smoother production flow in the future, it may be possible to reduce the figure for variable manufacturing overheads in the calculation. In this case it would probably be advisable to buy the component from the outside supplier.

The distinction between fixed and variable costs is important when assessing what information is relevant to these short-term tactical decisions. As we saw in our discussion of pricing policies (page 68) there are some occasions when it is acceptable to quote a price which only covers variable costs of production. Where accounting reports are prepared for managers who have to take these decisions, it is advisable to show clearly the distinction between fixed and variable costs in what is usually described as a 'marginal costing' presentation of the information (see Chapter 5).

In the previous case the production manager was faced with a simple alternative: whether to make or buy out the circuit board. In many situations there is a larger number of possible choices and the manager's task is to use the firm's limited resources in the best possible way. In these cases it will be necessary to employ techniques of operational research such as linear programming (page 88) to arrive at the optimum solution. When using these techniques, the principles governing the selection of data are the same as when making a simple comparison between a number of proposals. Future, differential costs should be included; sunk and common costs should be ignored.

The choice between making a component in the factory or buying from an outside supplier is a choice between current alternatives. Building a new factory or investing in expensive capital equipment involves a high initial cost which is unlikely to be justified unless we take into account the expected benefits from that investment over a number of years. Time is therefore an additional dimension in the appraisal of capital projects compared with short-term decisions of the 'make or buy out' type.

The only satisfactory methods of giving due allowance for the time element in these 'long run' decisions is by using the concept of discounting. The principle is quite simple. A pound today is worth more to me than a pound to be paid in one year's time. The preference for present cash rather than future cash can be expressed as a rate of discount. For instance, if a 10% rate of discount is assumed, £10 to be paid in one year's time has the equivalent value of £9.09 paid today, and £10 to be paid in two year's time is the equivalent of £8.26 today. Another way of expressing the same relationship is to say that the *present value* of £10 in two years' time is £8.26, given a discount rate of 10%.

One example of the use of discounting techniques is in ranking two capital proposals each with a different pattern of cash flow over time, by comparing the Net Present Value of each project. Let us assume that each alternative involves an initial outlay of £8,000. The estimated net cash flows (receipts less expenditure) for both projects are given in table 8.4.

Table 8.4 Estimated net cash flows of two alternative capital projects

Initial Outlay	Project A Net Cash Flow	Project B Net Cash Flow
	£	£
Initial Outlay	−8,000	−8,000
Year 1	5,000	3,000
Year 2	4,000	3,000
Year 3	3,000	3,000
Year 4	2,000	3,000
Year 5	1,000	3,000
Year 6	−	1,000

The next step is to calculate or assume the 'cost of capital' of the business. This is expressed as a rate of return and may be based on the actual rates which the company pays when raising long-term capital. On the other hand, it may be an 'opportunity cost' based on the return which the company could have obtained if it were to invest in a similar project having similar risks.

Let us assume that the cost of capital in our example is 16%. Tables are published showing the present value of £1, at different rates of discount. If the 16% discount factor is applied to the information in table 8.4 we may obtain the discounted cash flow (DCF) for each proposal (table 8.5).

Table 8.5 Discounted Cash Flows (16% rate of discount)

	Project A			Project B		
	Undis-counted net cash flow	Discount factor	Dis-counted net cash flow	Undis-counted net cash flow	Discount factor	Dis-counted net cash flow
Initial outlay	−8,000		−8,000	−8,000		−8,000
Year 1	5,000	0.86207	4,310	2,000	0.86207	1,724
Year 2	4,000	0.74316	2,973	3,000	0.74316	2,229
Year 3	3,000	0.64066	1,922	3,000	0.64066	1,922
Year 4	2,000	0.55229	1,105	3,000	0.55229	1,657
Year 5	1,000	0.47611	476	3,000	0.47611	1,428
Year 6				2,000	0.41044	821
Total	7,000		2,786	8,000		1,781

If we compare the undiscounted net cash flows of the two projects over their respective lives, it would appear that Project B (total £8,000) is a more attractive proposition than Project A (total £7,000). By discounting these cash flows at the appropriate rate, we will reach the opposite conclusion. The net present value of Project A is £2,786 whereas the net present value of Project B is only £1,781.

It is rare for a decision maker to be able to predict the results of his actions with complete certainty. In practice a manager must operate under conditions of uncertainty (where the probability of different possible outcomes is unknown) or risk (where it is possible to assign probabilities to these outcomes).

Let us assume that the company wishes to invest a substantial sum of money in a research and development project for an entirely new type of visual display unit. It is notoriously difficult to predict the cost of a research and development programme. When the research manager was first asked, his initial guess was that this project would cost £300,000 in total. Further consideration of all the factors enabled the research manager to refine this statement and express his prediction in probabilistic form:

There is a 30% chance that the project will cost £500,000.
There is a 60% chance that the project will cost £300,000.
There is a 10% chance that the project will cost £200,000.

By weighing each of the three outcomes by their respective probabilities, we may calculate the Expected Monetary Value (EMV) of the cost of this proposal:

$$EMV = (0.3 \times 500,000) + (0.6 \times 300,000) + (0.1 \times 200,000) = £350,000$$

In spite of all the difficulties involved in assigning realistic probabilities to each outcome, the EMV (£350,000) is likely to be a more satisfactory guide than the original guess (£300,000) when making a decision about whether to start the programme.

The subject of risk analysis is more complex than this example would suggest. For instance, the attitude of the decision maker in the above example would be different if it was estimated that the business would incur unacceptably heavy losses if the project were to cost £500,000 *and* if the subsequent sales of the product during the next two years were 50% below budget (there is a 20% probability of this happening). The probability of both these outcomes occurring together is 0.2 × 0.3 or 0.06. The company may decide that even a 6% chance of financial disaster is not worth taking.

This brief and rather superficial survey of decision accounting has touched on a wide range of principles, techniques and concepts including marginal costing, linear programming, risk analysis and discounting methods. There are many other possible mathematical models which may be used to formulate and solve business problems. The techniques of linear programming, for instance, are merely part of the wider study known as operational research (see Chapter 6). It is apparent that many of these methods require a greater mathematical expertise than is traditionally associated with the accountant's role as a recorder and reporter of financial and cost information. If the accountant is to be effective in providing relevant information for business decisions, he must be familiar with the quantitative techniques which have been introduced in this chapter.

CHAPTER 9

Government and Law

The idea that the modern business enterprise operates in a complex and sometimes 'turbulent' environment was first introduced in Chapter 3. A firm such as Small Print has direct contact with customers, suppliers and others but beyond these immediate relationships there are more general economic, social and political forces affecting the business. In discussing the functions of business (e.g. marketing, finance, personnel and production) we have frequently mentioned economic and social forces, but little has so far been said about the legal and political environment of business apart from noting the increasing influence of the state on business activity even in the 'capitalist' countries of the West. This chapter will examine this role of the state more closely. The two main themes will be the legal framework of business activity and the relationship between government and industry in the United Kingdom.

The Political System

The idea of the business enterprise as a complex system was introduced in the early part of this book. Rather than looking at the separate departments of the enterprise as defined by its formal organisation, we found it more convenient to consider such general relationships as the social system or the financial system of the business. This approach emphasises the broad functions of the whole business enterprise rather than the detailed structure and operation of particular departments.

It is possible to look at political systems in a similar manner. A study of the UK political system for instance, would probably start with a description of specialised 'political' institutions such as the House of Commons, the Cabinet, local authorities, the Civil Service and the political parties. However, a mere description of these institutions would have limited value if our main concern was to find out how the total political system actually works. For example, a description of the way in which political ideas are communicated in the UK would refer to the press and the broadcasting authorities as well as the more obviously 'political' organisations such as political parties.

A systems analysis of politics, like the systems approach to the study of business, attempts to explain how various system inputs are converted into system outputs. There is no universally agreed classification of political inputs and outputs, and it would be folly to expect complete agreement given the widely differing views which may be held about the ends of political activity. Some writers would even doubt the validity of this type of systems theory; whether it attempts to explain business, politics or any other complex social activity. Some of these doubts are reviewed in the final chapter of this book.

It is no part of our present brief to develop such a general systems theory of politics; our concern is simply to identify political inputs and outputs which are clearly relevant to an understanding of business activity in the UK. There are a number of difficulties in accepting these limitations to the discussion, including the fact that in modern trading conditions, national boundaries are losing their significance. The political environment of a company registered in the UK might include supra-national organisations such as the European Economic Community, the political systems of countries in which it conducts foreign trade or has foreign subsidiaries, and local and regional government within the UK. The government's freedom of action may be limited by international monetary and trading agreements. Membership of the EEC means that many aspects of business, such as restrictive trade agreements, transport and labour policies are subject to Community Law, which could in some cases override UK law. The present discussion is limited to the policies of the UK central government, but the significance of this limitation will be seen if we remember that the countries in which Small Print operates have widely different political systems and varying degrees of political stability.

So far as the business world is concerned, the most important inputs to the political system take the form of numerous and often conflicting demands for government action. In the period preceding the Budget, for instance, the TUC, the CBI, professional associations and sectional groups such as the Automobile Association, will press their views on the Chancellor of the Exchequer. The CBI may ask for a reduction in the higher marginal rates of income tax to provide incentives for management; the TUC might prefer a reduction in indirect taxation such as the Value Added Tax which would reduce the general cost of living. The government might be under pressure from the construction industry to increase public building programmes and so reduce the rate of unemployed in the industry. Pressure groups often try to persuade government to take action which would have a direct effect on business operations. The anti-smoking lobby campaigns for a reduction in the advertising expenditure of cigarette manufacturers; conservation groups argue for an extension of pollution control measures which will increase costs of production in certain industries; consumer groups press for higher standards of quality, safety and service.

Business pressure groups may represent a locality (local Chamber of Commerce), an industry (e.g. Engineering Employer's Association) or business interests in general (Confederation of British Industry). As the CBI and the TUC stand at the apex of this system of economic representation their advice is often sought when government wishes to consult 'the two sides of industry'. This wide representation can also be a source of weakness, however. In 1974, the CBI had over 11,000 companies in membership and claimed to represent large companies, nationalised industries and small businesses. How effective is the CBI in speaking for these diverse interests? A recent study of the influence that the CBI was able to exert on legislation passing through Parliament came to the following conclusion: 'The general picture that emerges is that the CBI is able to influence the details of legislation in a way which can benefit its members, but that it has relatively little influence on general government policies.' (Grant and Marsh 1975, page 94).

The power of the state is expressed in different ways: through legislation, administrative or executive action and judicial decisions. These three types of activity may be said to be *outputs* of the political system. The idea of a three-fold classification of the powers of government was originally associated with Montesquieu's belief* that liberty would be best preserved if different persons or groups of persons shared the functions of government, although this condition was not fully satisfied by the British constitution of the eighteenth century which Montesquieu held up as a model. At the present time it would be more accurate to describe the British constitution in terms of the concentration of powers in the hands of the Prime Minister and his Cabinet, rather than the Separation of Powers of Montesquieu's doctrine. The enormous tasks which modern governments take upon themselves have led to an inevitable concentration of power in the hands of the state.

How are these immense powers of government used to influence and control business activity? It will be convenient to discuss the issues in two stages. We will first examine the relationship between business and the executive arm of government in a modern industrial state. We then look at the legal framework of business and consider some important business relationships in their legal context. It is clearly impossible to do more than scratch the surface of these important matters. In introducing this discussion of the political and legal environment of business in the UK, it is perhaps necessary to underline the warning that 'a little learning is a dangerous thing'.

* Montesquieu's book, *De L'Esprit des Lois,* was published in 1748.

Government and Business

As we saw in Chapter 3, even the classical doctrine of laissez-faire allowed an important though limited role to the state. External defence and the preservation of law and order are essential if business is to thrive. Without a secure and stable business environment, businessmen will be unwilling to enter into long-term commitments. It was also accepted by enlightened opinion that the state had a moral duty to intervene in a clear case of oppression of the weak. The growth of factory legislation in the nineteenth century shows how this principle would be used to justify regulation by the state of the activities of manufacturing businesses.

Factory owners in the late eighteenth century were subject to no legal restraint on the way they treated their workers apart from the general criminal law. Young children could work long hours in badly ventilated factories operating dangerous machinery. The prevailing view at the time was that the specific regulation of these matters was not the proper concern of the law. Gradually public opinion changed and in a succession of statutes throughout the nineteenth century, the hours of work of children, young persons and women were regulated, certain dangerous trades were made illegal and dangerous machinery was required to be fenced. One of these measures, the Factory Act of 1833, took the important step of permitting the appointment of factory inspectors to ensure that this legislation was properly enforced. Minimum standards continued to be raised and the scope of protection was extended. The Health and Safety at Work Act 1974, which is the latest in this line of statutes, consolidates the legislation relating to employees generally; the earlier Factories Acts only protected factory workers.

The boundary between matters which are thought to be the proper concern of government intervention and the many different social, economic, moral and political reasons for or against such intervention continue to be matters of fierce political debate. One thing is certain, however. There has been a tendency in recent years for the state to assume wider and more onerous economic responsibilities, and for intervention in the organisation, control and finance of business to increase.

It would be an impossible task to catalogue the full extent of this involvement; the influence of the state pervades every aspect of business activity. In his book *Government and Industry*, J.W. Grove attempted to chart the full extent of this relationship as it appeared in 1960. It is perhaps significant that no one has undertaken the Herculean task of bringing the story up to date; one obvious difficulty is that any survey would be out of date before the printer's ink had dried.

The framework used by Grove for the presentation of his detailed account of the relationship between government and industry is still relevant today. The exact nature of the relationship varies with the circumstances; the government may adopt the role of *regulator, promoter, entrepreneur* or *planner* as occasion demands. Table 9.1 is a modified version of Grove's analysis with a limited number of examples to illustrate each of the above categories. The reader is advised to study the activities of government in more detail, either by following references to these examples or by looking at other cases of government intervention in the current press. What is the extent of the powers given to the government under an Act of Parliament — the Industry Act (1975), for expample? What policies are currently being followed by a government department or agency? What were the social, political and economic reasons for a particular case of government intervention?

It is clear from such an analysis that the relationship between government and industry is far more complex than is implied by the common division of the economy into the 'public' and 'private' sectors. It is usual to define the 'public sector' as that part of the economy over which the state has direct control — the state's role as *entrepreneur*. This would include the provision of 'public' services such as defence, internal security, and the protection of the physical environment; the provision of certain personal services such as education and medical care by collective action as an alternative to provision by market forces; and the production by 'nationalised industries' of goods and services such as rail and air transport, coal, electricity, gas, iron and steel, which are generally sold on the market in the same way that a 'private'

Table 9.1 Government and Industry (after Grove 1960)

Government as regulator	*Examples*
The regulation of economic organisation	Licensing of transport undertakings Powers of the National Enterprise Board under the Industry Act (1975)
The control of monopoly and restrictive practices	Fair Trading Act (1973): (i) Registration of restrictive trade practices (ii) Reports of the Monopolies and Mergers Commission
Consumer protection	(iii) Powers of the Director General of Fair Trading Consumer Consultative Councils of public corporations
The regulation of wages and conditions of work	Protection under statutes: Health and Safety at Work Act 1974 Employment Protection Act 1975 Wages Councils Act 1959

Government as promoter	
Provision of finance, subsidies, grants and information	Subsidies and grants under the Industry Act 1972: Industrial and Commercial Finance Corporation Finance Corporation for Industry Small Firms Information Centres
Promotion of research	National Research and Development Corporation Government sponsored research laboratories, e.g. National Physical Laboratory Science Research Council
Promotion of good industrial relations and industrial democracy	Conciliation Service of the Department of Employment, Industrial Tribunals.
Protection of domestic industries	By tariffs, import quotas and negotiations with foreign countries (e.g. Japan). There are international agreements which limit the scope for this protection, (e.g. GATT)

Promotion of overseas trade	See text (page 142)
Employment services, training and education	The Employment Services Agency - Job Centres The Training Services Agency - the Training Opportunities Scheme The provision of vocational education and training in universities, polytechnics and colleges of further education

Government as entrepreneur

Government as purchaser, employer, producer and trader	Public corporations, e.g.
	    National Coal Board
	    British Airways
	    Atomic Energy Authority
	    Post Office
	National Enterprise Board shareholdings, e.g.
	    International Computers Ltd
	    Rolls Royce (1971) Ltd
	    British Leyland Motor Corporation Ltd
	By 1981 about 1 in 5 of the working population will be employed in public services (see page 29)
	Government purchases of materials and services, e.g.
	    Public buildings programmes
	    Military equipment

Government as planner

The machinery of planning	National Economic Development Council (general policies) Economic Development Committees (separate industries)
Regional planning	Regional Economic Councils and Planning Boards Development Areas Industrial Development Certificates Regional Employment Premiums
Regulation of aggregate demand in the economy by fiscal and monetary measures	See text (page 142)

company such as ICI sells its products. However, as Grove's analysis shows, the so-called 'private sector' is subject to detailed regulation by the state of much of its activities: wages, conditions of work, industrial safety, product quality, prices, methods of trading, and credit terms are merely a few of the matters which may be subject to government regulations.

In addition to the 'stick' of regulation, there is also the 'carrot' of promotion. For example, a number of agencies have been established by government. The Export Credits Guarantee Department will insure an exporter against the possibility of default by an overseas buyer, thus reducing some of the risks of exporting. The British Overseas Trade Board, with the assistance of other government agencies, offers a wide range of services to a firm such as Small Print which wishes to develop its export markets. These include *inter alia*

Market assessments
Information on tariffs and import regulations
Assistance with overseas business visits
Help in finding an agent or representative
Information on the commercial standing of overseas traders
Protecting the commercial interests of British firms abroad
Support for displays at overseas trade fairs and exhibitions
Advice on documentation procedures
Help with market research
Advice on financing exports
Export Handbook

Above all, the modern state regulates total demand in the economy in order to stimulate economic growth and to reduce the sharp fluctuations between boom and slump which were a feature of economic life before the Second World War. In 1936, John Maynard Keynes in his *General Theory of Employment Interest and Money* outlined a theory of aggregate demand which suggested ways in which capitalist economies could be helped to meet their objectives. Today governments have a whole armoury of economic weapons at their disposal: fiscal policies (e.g. a reduction in indirect taxation to stimulate private consumption); monetary policies (e.g. a reduction of interest rates to stimulate company investment); prices and incomes policies; physical controls (e.g. import regulation by tariffs and quotas); and the regulation of public expenditure.

The object of government economic management in a basically capitalist economy is to provide a favourable environment for economic growth. Government economic planning is intended to supplement the internal plans of individual business enterprises. The marketing plans of a car company will assume a certain level of purchasing power in the economy. There is no point in mounting an expensive advertising campaign to persuade the public to buy a new car model unless enough people will be able to afford it. General economic uncertainty can have a harmful effect on company sales: a widespread fear of unemployment might discourage potential car buyers from taking on additional financial commitments.

In Galbraith's view (1967) the fate of the large business corporation is so closely linked to government policies that it would be more realistic to see both as part of a single industrial system — 'the New Industrial State'.

> No sharp line separates government from the private firm; the line becomes very indistinct and even imaginary. Each organisation is important to the other, members are intermingled in their daily work; each organisation comes to accept the other's goals; each adapts the goals of the other to its own. Each organisation, accordingly, is an extension of the other. The large aerospace contractor is related to the Air Force by ties that, however different superficially, are in their substance the same as those that relate the Air Force to the United States Government. Shared goals are the decisive links in each case. (Galbraith 1967, page 317)

Many aspects of Galbraith's thesis have been criticised by economists. Perhaps large business corporations are not as self-perpetuating and as immune from market forces as he suggests. His argument relates to those business corporations which 'form the heart of the industrial system' — the two hundred largest corporations in the United States. A medium-sized company such as Small Print could hardly be said to be part of 'the New Industrial State' even though it is involved in advanced technology. Perhaps this concept is a striking journalistic phrase which is difficult to define in practice. In spite of these difficulties, Galbraith's book remains a persuasive description of the close relationship between government and big business in an advanced industrial economy.

Business and the Law

The relationship between law, custom and morality has been the subject of unending speculation by philosophers and legal theorists since at least the time of the ancient Greeks. What are the appropriate limits to the use of the law to regulate various areas of human activity such as business? How does the law respond to changing social and economic forces? Rather than discuss these difficult questions in general terms, we shall examine specific business situations which may help to explain the role of law in a modern industrial society.

The law cannot ensure that all our actions spring from the highest motives but it can intervene if our conduct falls below certain minimum standards. As we have already noted, certain standards of health, safety and welfare in workplaces are laid down by law. A company may, of course, provide better facilities if it wishes but it is only the minimum standards that are enforceable by law.

It is easy to exaggerate the power of the law to encourage morality. Measures such as the Race Relations Act 1968 and the Sex Discrimination Act 1975 may help to mould public opinion through the clear statement that certain actions are against the law, but it is difficult to change deeply rooted attitudes merely by passing an Act of Parliament.

Some legal rules do not have a specifically 'moral' content:

The Daily Globe has been negotiating with Small Print for the purchase of a phototypesetter model B39 with certain special modifications. On 10 January the Daily Globe writes to Small Print offering to buy the equipment at a price of £52,000. Small Print accepts the offer by letter on 14 January stating that the order will be scheduled for immediate production. Unfortunately the letter of acceptance is lost in the post and after a month has elapsed the Daily Globe construes that Small Print has lost interest in the negotiations and orders a similar phototypesetter from Gutenberg. Small Print produces the special order but the Daily Globe refuses to accept delivery as it now feels obliged to wait for the Gutenberg equipment.

A legally binding contract comes into existence when a definite offer is unconditionally accepted by the other party. In this case, the Daily Globe's letter of 10 January is a definite offer and Small Print's letter of 14 January is an unconditional acceptance. It is a rule of English law that where it is reasonable to accept an offer by post, the acceptance is complete as soon as the letter of acceptance is posted whether it reaches its destination or not. The two parties have therefore entered into a binding contract and so Small Print will be able to sue for damages arising from the breach of contract.

The reader will notice that 'moral' issues hardly arise in this case. The Post Office may be to blame for the loss of the letter but it is not legally liable in such cases. A moment's consideration should convince the reader that if the Post Office were generally liable for losses arising out of their negligence in handling the mail, there would be enormous difficulties of proof and the Post Office would be over-whelmed with trivial and vexatious litigation which would necessarily add to the cost of the service. On balance it is in the public interest that the Post Office's liability is restricted to cases where extra payment has been made by the customer to insure against loss as may be done through the recorded delivery service.

The legal solution to our problem must therefore entail a choice as to which of the two 'innocent' parties to the contract will suffer as a result of the lost letter. The actual result may seem unfair on the Daily Globe which feels that it has a moral obligation to Gutenberg. If, on the other hand, the acceptance by post was only effective when the letter was received by the Daily Globe, this would seem equally unfair on Small Print which incurred considerable expense on the special order. Many rules of law are concerned with convenience and certainty rather than morality. The overriding requirement in this and similar cases is that there should be a clear rule which determines the precise point at which a binding contract is made. It is particularly important for businessmen to 'know where they stand'.

In business terms, the case of Small Print v The Daily Globe is a dispute between seller and customer; in legal terms it is an example of a contractual obligation. A distinction must therefore be drawn between the various business relationships (e.g. employer—employee, company—shareholder, seller—purchaser, the business and government) and the basic legal categories of *contract, tort* and *crime*. The rights and duties arising out of each separate business relationship must be expressed in terms of one or more of these legal concepts.

The nature of these three types of legal action may be illustrated through an examination of the *seller—customer* relationship. The Daily Globe case is a good example of a legally binding *contract* between two parties for the sale of goods. Either party may sue the other in respect of any breach of the terms of the contract. The party bringing the action, or plaintiff, would usually be asking the court for an award of damages in compensation for any loss which he may have suffered as a result of the defendant's breach. The Daily Globe case is one of a direct agreement between seller and purchaser, but we have seen that much of Small Print's export trade is carried out indirectly through overseas agents acting on the company's behalf. Small Print would be bound by an agreement between such an agent and a third party as if the company had dealt with the customer direct.

It is not always possible to infer a contractual relationship between a seller and the ultimate consumer of the product. Let us suppose that a manufacturer M, sells a product to a retailer R, who sells it to a customer C, who then gives the product to a friend Z. M's product has a hidden defect and as a result Z suffers injury whilst using it. It is not possible for Z to bring an action for breach of contract against M, R, or C because there is no contract between Z and any of these parties. The important case of *Donoghue v Stevenson* (1932) laid down the principle that in similar circumstances Z could bring an action for the *tort* (or civil wrong) of negligence against M if it could be proved that the existence of the defect was M's fault. Z's action for damages will be based on the breach of a duty to take care which the manufacturer owes to the ultimate consumer rather than any breach of contract.

There are certain cases where a sale to a customer can give rise to *criminal* proceedings: the unauthorised sale of a dangerous drug, a sale which contravenes the Exchange Control regulations or a sale which has been obtained as a result of a false trade description to give but three of many possible examples. There is a crucial difference between criminal and civil actions. The purpose of a civil action is to enable one party to obtain a remedy for any loss or injury he has suffered whether the damage arises from a tort such as negligence or a breach of contract. A criminal prosecution on the other hand is conducted on behalf of the state and if the case against the defendant is proved, the court may impose a penalty such as a fine or imprisonment.

Let us now turn to the *employer—employee* relationship. Whenever a worker is hired he enters into a contract of employment with his employer. The contract itself need not be in writing but the employer is bound to give written notice to the employee of the more important terms of the contract. These 'written particulars' must cover such matters as holiday entitlement, the minimum period of notice, job title, pension provision, if any, and arrangements for sick pay.* In most cases, the duties of the employee will not be formally stated but the general law implies that he should obey lawful orders, use reasonable care and skill in carrying out his work and be loyal and faithful to his employer. The employer has a duty to pay the agreed wages; he is also under an obligation to provide safe premises, a safe system of work and safe equipment for his employees.

A worker who has been injured because his employer has failed to meet these standards of safety may sue his employer to obtain compensation for the financial loss which he has suffered (e.g. loss of earnings). Apart from an action for damages the worker may have a right to industrial injuries benefit under the national insurance scheme to which all employees must contribute. These benefits are at a fixed rate and so, considered by themselves, would not necessarily compensate the worker for the financial loss he had suffered as a result of the injury. On the other hand, it is not necessary to prove that the employer has been negligent in order to claim industrial benefits; the employee has merely to show that he was injured as a result of an 'accident arising out of and in the course of his employment' (Social Security Act 1975).

This brief account of the law relating to injuries at work

* Contracts of Employment Act 1972 and Employment Protection Act 1975

shows an intricate pattern of rights and duties between employer, employee and the State. In practice, there may be further complications to be resolved. What is the legal position if the employee has been partly to blame for his injuries? Will the court take account of any industrial injuries benefit to which the employee might be entitled when assessing damages arising from an action for negligence? How strict is the duty of an employer towards his employee? Is it enough that the employer provides safety equipment such as goggles to protect the worker against eye injuries, or must the employer also insist that the safety goggles are worn?

The law has to strike a balance between various conflicting interests and the relative influence of different social pressures will change over time. In recent years, for instance, there have been strong pressures to give the worker more protection against unfair dismissal and to increase job security in general. The Trade Union and Labour Relations Act 1974 and the Employment Protection Act 1975 have altered the balance of interest between employer and employee significantly in favour of the employee. A similar tendency to protect the ordinary citizen from the power of big business can be seen in the law relating to the sale of goods. For instance, the Consumer Credit Act 1974 is designed to provide a comprehensive code covering hire purchase, consumer credit and related matters under the supervision of the Director General of Fair Trading. Many of its provisions strengthen the legal rights of the credit consumer and restrict the activities of businesses offering consumer credit (e.g. control of advertisements for credit facilities, licensing of those carrying on a consumer credit business).

The shifting balance of power between different interest groups appears most sharply in the law relating to business enterprises. The basic position arises from the principle of company law that directors must only act in the interests of the shareholder members of the company.

> It is apparently only the interests of the members, present and future to which they are entitled to have regard; the interests of the employees, the consumers of the company's products or the nation as a whole are legally irrelevant. (Gower 1969, page 522)

In practice, all these interests must be served if the company is to continue in business and prosper. Unfortunately, legal difficulties may arise when a company is about to cease trading. In the case of *Parke v. Daily News Ltd* (1962) two newspapers owned by the defendant company had been sold, and under the terms of the sale the purchasing company did not assume any liability for pensions or compensation to employees made redundant as a result of the take-over. The directors felt morally bound to make certain *ex gratia* payments to these staff and pensioners but a shareholder (Parke) brought an action to test the legality of these proposed payments. In deciding in favour of the plaintiff shareholder the judge said:

> The defendants were prompted by motives which, however laudable, and however enlightened from the point of view of industrial relations, were such as the law does not recognise as sufficient justification. . . The directors of the defendant company are proposing that a very large part of its funds should be given to its former employees in order to benefit those employees rather than the company, and that is an application of the company's funds which the law, as I understand it, will not allow . . .*

Although the decision in *Parke v. Daily News* gives priority to the rights of shareholders, recent proposals for company law reform and discussions of the responsibilities of company directors tend to stress the interests of other groups.

Two examples of the prevailing trend must suffice. The Accounting Standards Steering Committee in a document entitled *The Corporate Report* (1975) has argued that in addition to their minimum legal responsibilities to shareholders, companies have a wider social responsibility to the community. The report mentions equity shareholders, loan creditors, employees, investment analysts and advisers, business contacts, government and the general public as separate groups each with a valid interest in the future of the company. Each of these groups has particular information needs and it is recommended that company reporting techniques should be developed to meet these wider requirements.

In addition to these demands for more disclosure of

* per Plowman, J., 1962, 2 All E.R. 948

company information, there have been powerful demands for worker participation and industrial democracy. However, in spite of wide general acceptance of the need for some movement in this direction, there is considerable debate about the form that employee participation should take. Lord Bullock's Committee of Inquiry on Industrial Democracy (1977) was unable to agree on a single recommendation for government action; whether, for instance, workers should be represented directly or through trade unions. Whatever measure of participation is eventually introduced, there will undoubtedly be a shift in the balance of power between shareholders, senior management, workers and trade unions in the larger companies.

CHAPTER 10

The Study of Business

Our brief survey of business activity is now concluded. This final chapter reviews some of the themes that have been introduced earlier in the book. As well as looking back to these earlier discussions we shall be looking forward to ways in which the subject may be studied in greater depth. At this stage, therefore, the emphasis will be on the strengths and limitations of different approaches to the study of business rather than the content of such studies.

The earlier part of this book adopted a simple systems framework for presenting this rich diversity of material which we call 'business'. Technical, social, financial and information systems were identified within the enterprise and with the help of an extended case study these business systems were examined in relation to the firm's immediate and general environment. In later chapters, various business functions such as marketing, production, personnel and finance were discussed in more detail and we examined the impact of government and law on business activities.

The study of business is an attempt to find regularities, patterns and meanings in all these activities. Given this diversity of material we would expect to meet a number of different strategies for the analysis of business and business behaviour. We have already encountered academic disciplines (economics, psychology, sociology, political science, mathematics), interdisciplines such as organisation theory, the study of business functions (marketing, production, finance) and management techniques (work study and network analysis). Each of these studies tells us something important about business without giving a complete picture of 'business'. In this respect, the study of business is no different from the study of other fields of human activity such as engineering, medicine, town planning and education. Practitioners in all these fields meet a wide range of problems and must handle different types of data. The doctor and the manager have one thing in common: they must each have acquired a grounding in several disciplines and interdisciplines, and be familiar with a number of techniques if they are to cope effectively with all the problems which they meet in their professional life.

Academic Disciplines and Business

Our familiarity with the idea of academic subjects stretches back to our early schooldays, and our first acquaintance with the 'three Rs' and periods in the time-table set aside for activities called 'geography' and 'history'. Because we grow up with the idea of separate academic disciplines there is a tendency to take them for granted as part of the natural order of things. Among education theorists, however, fierce controversy rages about the nature and value of academic study through the traditional disciplines. At one extreme is the view that academic disciplines are the means 'whereby the whole of experience has become intelligible to man, they are the fundamental achievement of mind' (Hirst 1965). At the other extreme is the view that much of what passes for academic scholarship is valueless, at least as a guide for future action. 'The academic idiom was established to preserve the past, not to look forward to and create the future' (de Bono 1972).

There is even uncertainty in the name given to these studies. In referring to economics and sociology as subjects, we are emphasising content, the subject matter to be studied; if, on the other hand, we speak about disciplines, our attention is directed to different styles of thinking and methods of analysis. When economics is called the 'science of wealth' we are defining the subject matter which we intend to study: the laws governing the production and consumption of goods and services. Other definitions might emphasise procedures and concepts, as in Robbins' classic statement that economics is about 'the allocation of scarce means towards competing ends'.

The Role of Theory

Each academic discipline abstracts certain types of data from the universe of possible facts and applies specialised methods of analysis to those data. Thus, economists define the economic 'facts' which interest them and concentrate their attention on describing relationships between these variables, whilst assuming that all other non-economic variables may be held constant for the purpose of analysis. The analysis of demand as presented in Chapter 5 will serve as an illustration of this method. Similarly, sociologists, political scientists, historians and other specialists will make their own selection of facts in the light of current views about what data are relevant for their study.

These various enterprises which we call academic disciplines are, in their different ways, attempts to see patterns in the mass of observed data — laws in the physical sciences or trends in history. A valid theory enables us to economise effort by bringing together a mass of detail into a more concise general statement; this is the truth behind the paradox that 'there is nothing so practical as a sound theory'. There is considerable variation between disciplines both in the generality of these statements and the confidence with which they are held. For instance, concepts such as 'the industrial revolution' may be useful shorthand symbols to express general historical trends but they can be misleading unless used with extreme caution. Unlike theories in the physical sciences which can be refuted by a single contrary instance, there are bound to be many exceptions to a general historical trend. The survival of hand-loom weavers well into the nineteenth century does not necessarily disprove the view that there was a dramatic change towards factory methods of production in the textile industries in the late eighteenth century.

Many of the most important debates within the business disciplines are about the validity of general statements. Is it possible to speak of a general theory of the firm or must the large corporation be treated differently from the classical entrepreneurial firm? Is it possible to develop a general theory of organisations which has relevance to business firms, hospitals and religious organisations? A theory which is too general is a distortion of reality, whereas a simple description of events without any attempt at analysis is both ephemeral and trivial. It is often a difficult task to find the appropriate level of generalisation to suit a particular problem. It is relatively easy to describe the machinery of collective bargaining in the UK at a particular date but much more difficult to formulate a valid general theory of industrial relations.

When we examine the form and purpose of these general statements it is clear that the role of theory varies between disciplines and between different traditions within a discipline. The most important of these distinctions is between positive theories which claim to make statements about what *is* and normative theories which make statements about what *ought to be.* In the twentieth century the most influential tradition of positivism has been in philosophy. According to the logical positivists, a valid statement in philosophy or science must be expressed in a form which is capable of verification. The statement that a particular company has made a million pounds' profit is expressed in an acceptable form as it is possible to bring evidence either to refute or confirm the statement. On the other hand, the statement that it is wicked to make excessive profits is, strictly speaking, nonsense. Such statements about values and norms are merely expressions of opinion which may be interesting and of practical importance in our everyday lives, but are not the proper concern of science.

The distinction between positive and normative theories is of crucial importance in economics. Positive economics makes statements about the working of the economic system in such a way that they may be tested against the facts of the real economic world. It should then be possible to make predictions about future economic events. Welfare economics, on the other hand, is concerned with policy rather than predictions. Starting from certain assumptions, which are in effect value judgments about how an economic system ought to be organised, the welfare economist assesses the policy implications of an economic proposal such as a change in the tax system or a major capital investment project such as the Channel Tunnel. Concepts such as justice and efficiency will never be proved to be true or false, but this does not necessarily mean that the concepts are meaningless.

Unfortunately, in recent years, the prestige of positive science and the attempts to create a 'value-free' social science have meant that normative discussions are somewhat out of fashion. This tendency to eliminate value judgments from analysis may mean that values are never properly considered when policy is being formulated.

We all have to make value judgments in our daily life and if we are to study an important field of human action such as business, it seems important to discuss the goals of that activity as well as trying to understand how the system works in order to make predictions. Advertising, customer relations, industrial relations, employment practices and pollution control are only a few of the areas where business decisions have a strong ethical content.

Although there is a growing interest in such moral questions and considerable debate about business objectives, most 'normative' management literature is concerned with means rather than ends. Techniques such as work study and operational research set out rules which tell managers what they should do if they wish to achieve certain standards. Method study, for instance, is a procedure for examining work flows in the hope of eliminating wasteful activities. In operational research a complex business problem is expressed in mathematical terms to derive the optimum solution to the problem. The aim of operational research is to develop models which will help managers make more rational decisions. In effect, the exponents of these techniques are saying to managers 'if you want to achieve certain goals this is what you must do'. Efficiency is the end and management science provides the means.

Disciplines and Interdisciplines

We have seen that each academic discipline makes its own simplifying assumptions about reality because it is only by holding some of the variables constant that the problem becomes manageable. Unfortunately there will be many business problems which can only be analysed within the framework of a single academic discipline at the risk of serious distortion of the facts. It was clear from our discussion of industrial relations (Chapter 7) that the subject cannot be reduced to either a branch of economics or a branch of sociology; it is a multi-faceted problem. In cases like this, we may adopt one of two possible approaches.

Multi-disciplinary studies bring together the separate contributions of a number of disciplines to a problem or field of study. For example, the problem of industrial relations may be examined through the contribution of industrial law, labour economics and industrial sociology in turn. The hope is that these perspectives will complement each other so that a more complete picture is gained than would be possible through a single-discipline study.

Unfortunately this method is not always successful. An understanding of industrial relations requires more than an appreciation of various 'aspects' of the problem. As in the story of the five blind men who each tried to describe the elephant, but only succeeded in describing its trunk, tail etc., there is a risk of concentrating on matters which, however important in themselves, are peripheral to the core of the problem. Early studies of industrial relations in the UK leaned heavily on descriptions of the machinery for collective bargaining, the history of the trade union movement and the law relating to trade unions. Without denying the importance of these matters, a fundamental analysis of the nature of industrial conflict needed to progress beyond a mere description of the legal, historical and institutional background of industrial relations. Complex models including social, psychological and economic variables would be needed to explain the relationship between various aspects of the problem. The achievement of this kind of synthesis is the aim of *interdisciplinary studies*. Here the intention is to create new concepts which cut across traditional boundaries of academic study.

Within the broad field of business studies, there are three main groups of interdisciplinary or multi-disciplinary studies.

1. Studies of specialist business *functions*

Personnel management, financial management and similar studies each provide a range of insights into a particular business function as a guide to more efficient management. They are therefore *applied* studies drawing on many sources and offering a number of different perspectives. As we saw in Chapter 5, the study of marketing draws heavily on the disciplines of economics, psychology, sociology and statistics. There are also a number of concepts which may be said to belong entirely to the subject of marketing — the idea of marketing mix, for example.

2. Studies of complex business *problems*

In describing the activities of Small Print, we identified four separate systems: the technical, social, financial and information systems. At first sight it might appear that most business problems could be neatly assigned to one of these separate systems and studied by the appropriate specialist. We might, for instance, make the assumption that sociologists and psychologists are only concerned with problems arising within the social system.

Closer examination shows that the true situation is more complex. The 'systems' of the business should not be studied in isolation but visualised as a group of overlapping circles. Many of the most interesting and intractable problems of business management occur within the areas of intersection of these circles. The design of production methods using the concept of the 'socio-technical system' and the effect of a budgetary control system on the motivation of supervisors and managers are examples of problems which cut across these artificial systems boundaries. In such cases an interdisciplinary or multi-disciplinary analysis is essential.

3. Studies of relevant *concepts*

It is not easy to describe business activities without using such words as 'decision', 'information', 'organisation' and 'system'. These concepts are not the exclusive concern of business but it is clear that the advanced student of business will need to assess the relevance of such studies as decision theory, cybernetics, information theory and general system theory to business management. These studies, which are themselves inter-related, bring together many strands of research. There are, for instance, a number of approaches in small-group sociology, social psychology and the sociology of organisations which may be applied in an analysis of relationships within primary groups or within the business organisation itself. Organisation theory attempts to draw together some of the ideas from these various sources. Other interdisciplinary studies might take ideas from mathematics, economics, engineering and even biology.

It is beyond our scope to examine these studies in any detail, but as we have made a number of references to open systems in the early chapters of the book, we shall take a closer look at the contribution of general systems theory to the study of business.

Systems Theory and Business

The main characteristic of systems thinking is a concern with relationships between a number of variables in terms of a total system; for instance, the circulation of the blood may be described as a system in which the individual elements such as the heart, veins and arteries each perform a function within the total system. It is, of course, possible to describe systems in almost any field of human activity. Throughout the presentation of the Small Print case study we identified a number of separate systems and sub-systems within the company, which could itself be defined as a system. In each case we observed a set of related elements working towards a goal or system objective. Through the marketing information system, for instance, data is researched, classified and processed, and information reported to management with the objective of improving the quality of marketing decisions. In general terms a system may be seen as a process whereby various inputs are converted to outputs which are intended to meet the system objective.

General systems theorists attempt to discover general principles which would be applicable to many different types of systems. The concepts of general systems theory have been applied in many diverse fields of study including biology, engineering, ecology, urban planning, psychology and politics (see Chapter 9) amongst many others. However, some of the more ambitious claims of systems theorists to have found a powerful unifying concept for general application have not been universally accepted. At a more modest level, many of the ideas emerging from these interdisciplinary comparisons have provided valuable insights of practical value in the design of actual production systems, information systems and the like.

As the machine is one of the simplest systems to understand, it is not surprising that the machine analogy has been used in a large number of systems studies. In our discussion of production systems (Chapter 6) we compared simple management control systems with a thermostat. In many business situations, however, the analogy of the machine is an oversimplification of reality. Business organisations are more *complex* than machines, they are *open* rather than closed systems and they have to *adapt* to their environment.

Let us look at these three characteristics in turn. In saying that the business firm is *complex* we are not merely drawing attention to the number of elements in the system. In the space age it is not difficult to find many examples of technologies which are much more complex than a simple thermostat. The point is rather that there are different *types* of interaction within the business system. In our description of Small Print, for instance, we found it necessary to identify separate technical, financial, information and social systems.

A closed system does not have relations with its environment apart from receiving inputs of energy, as when a watch is wound up and reset. It is an entirely passive relationship: unless the watch is continually rewound it will stop. On the other hand, the business enterprise is an *open* system drawing energy from its environment by its own action. The business enterprise takes in materials, services, finance and information from its environment, converts these inputs into products and services, and exports them to the environment as sales.

Open systems must be able to *adapt* to changes in the environment to survive. Plants and animals adapt to changes in their environment through a process of gradual evolutionary change; social systems must adjust more rapidly to changes in their environment. In the case of a business enterprise, this process of adaptation may force it to adopt an entirely new strategy, whether it be expansion, diversification, specialisation, consolidation or contraction. In Chapter 3 we examined the main aspects of the business environment in two stages: the immediate environment of an enterprise and more general social, economic and political influences on its activities. Open-systems theory enables us to go some way beyond a mere *description* of the environment towards an analysis of different types of environment and their relation to the enterprise. Open-systems studies have generated a number of concepts which may be used to analyse a business problem and suggest possible solutions. Emery and Trist's (1965) idea of a turbulent environment will serve as an example (page 25). In a complex business situation, general systems theory provides a fruitful way of thinking about the processes at work in the enterprise and its environment.

Apart from the analysis of complex business problems, systems concepts may be applied to the design and control of business systems such as quality control, stock control and production control systems. Ergonomics is the study of man/machine systems such as an aircraft instrumentation system. As the objective of such studies is to ensure that the human and the engineering elements work together as a total system, ergonomics draws from general systems concepts as well as from engineering and psychology. The design of management information systems is another example of the application of general systems concepts to a practical problem of business operation. The growing importance of the computer as a device for processing data has been the main impetus to this work. In our discussion of the Small Print case, we saw the importance of accurate, relevant information in taking operational and strategic decisions. As an organisation becomes more complex and its environment more turbulent, more energy must be devoted to the processing of information. Indeed, the very survival of the business may depend on the efficiency of its management information system.

Although systems theory is able to give valuable insights into business behaviour and help in such practical matters as the design of management information systems, we must beware of the uncritical use of the systems approach particularly in analysing business activity. It is easy to fall into the trap of treating a system as though it were a real entity with purposes of its own. We cannot see or touch a technical system; we can only describe it as an abstract concept. The idea has a value if it helps us to gain an insight into the working of business or helps us to solve practical problems, but it has no independent existence. The manager of an assembly line in a motor car factory may define the purpose of the production system for which he is responsible in fairly precise terms (the workers may see it rather differently); the system itself can have no purpose. If systems are merely logical constructions to help in the analysis of complex situations, it follows that there can be no universally applicable classification of systems and sub-systems of the business enterprise. In describing Small Print and its business environment, a particular model was used because it seemed appropriate for our purpose of introducing a mass of diverse material in a manageable form. Other classifications of systems and sub-systems might be appropriate if the purpose was different.

An important factor in deciding which particular systems classification to adopt is the standpoint to be taken by the investigation. Most systems models of business organisations, and indeed the model which has been used in this book, take the standpoint of management. However, as Burns (1966) has argued, we may describe the same social system from a number of different viewpoints. Management would define the business as a working organisation but it is also possible to analyse the political system and the career structure of the same organisation. We can observe a number of separate and distinct systems rather than a single system with its related sub-systems.

A separate but closely related logical trap might be called 'the Pangloss fallacy'. In Voltaire's story, Dr Pangloss taught Candide a philosophy of optimism which he summarised in the maxim that 'everything is for the best in this best of all possible worlds'. Dr Pangloss saw a chain connecting all the many escapades and calamities which had befallen Candide in the past to his final state of peaceable contentment. There are modern systems theorists who seem to share the same outlook. Everything which is observed seems to make some contribution to the working of a system. The fact that the market research department of Small Print is not responsible to the Sales Director may be explained as an outcome of the 'organic' social system of the business, rather than an oddity based on a succession of historical accidents. The danger is that if everything can be 'explained' as part of the system, there is no incentive to correct anomalies.

Analysis and Action

Most of the contributions of the academic disciplines and interdisciplines which we have discussed so far have been concerned with analysing certain aspects of business activities in an attempt to make general statements about that activity. The aim may be to achieve a deeper understanding of forces (e.g. psychological studies of motivation) and relationships (e.g. systems theory) or to make predictions about the future (e.g. positive economics). Often the study will also involve an element of policy guidance as in an accounting analysis of investment decisions. Although these studies have obvious practical implications, the purpose of this academic research is usually to make statements about the working of aspects of the business system in general terms. The microeconomist attempts to formulate a *general* theory of the firm not simply a model which is only relevant to the working of Small Print.

There are therefore a number of important differences between the formulation of academic theories or models and the solution of actual business problems:

1. A business decision is a unique event whereas an academic theory claims to have general validity over a wide range of possible events.

2. Business decisions have often to be taken in conditions of uncertainty and on the basis of inadequate information. The academic research worker may also experience difficulty in obtaining data to test his hypothesis, but as the formulation of the problem is under his control, so are his criteria for the selection of relevant information. It is not possible to 'hold other things constant' in business.

3. An academic may isolate 'values' and exclude them from his analysis; in choosing between alternative courses of action the business man is forced to make value judgments.

4. A business decision has to be taken within a certain time-scale; a manager may be unable to wait until the facts become clearer. Academic debate may take place at a more leisurely pace and with appropriate caution about reaching conclusions which are not fully supported by the evidence.

How can we make the transition from analysis to action? What is the relationship between these general concepts derived from academic study and the complex practical problems of business? There is an apocryphal story of a young economics graduate, who on his first day at ICI asked to see the company's demand curve. It is not merely a question of applying a general rule to a particular case which is a clear instance of that rule. The phenomena of everyday business life do not always come readily packaged as 'motivation problems' or 'investment decisions'.

An analogy with the medical profession may help us to understand the subtlety of the relationship between academic study and diagnostic skills. Knowledge of anatomy, physiology and many other academic studies is clearly essential for a general understanding of the workings of the body, but when prescribing treatment for a patient the doctor will be following the recognised procedures of clinical practice rather than 'applying' his knowledge of the basic scientific disciplines directly. In making a diagnosis he will be looking for generally recognised syndromes or sets of concurrent symptoms which will provide evidence of disease for which he can prescibe an accepted course of treatment. The significance of these clinical practices can only be appreciated if the doctor has an understanding of their scientific basis, but in the routine of the surgery he will hardly be aware that he is applying this scientific knowledge.

In the practice of management there is a whole armoury of techniques, procedures and methods which are the equivalent of these clinical practices in medicine. Although techniques such as work study, network analysis and management-by-objectives seem fairly self-contained, neatly packaged methods for solving practical business problems, the manager needs to be aware of the assumptions and limitations of each method before applying it in practice.

In other cases, there is a close link between the management technique and the contributing academic discipline; so that the technique may be said to be an operational version of the discipline study. The relationship between accounting and economics is essentially of this type. For example, the technique of break-even analysis used by management accountants is a practical application of the economist's theoretical analysis of the relationships between costs and volume. The results of economic analysis might suggest ways in which the traditional presentation of the break-even chart may be improved, but the practical problems of collecting, analysing and presenting the information as a basis for management decision are the concern of the accountant. Accounting and economics were once described as the 'uncongenial twins' but there is a growing recognition of the complementary nature of the two studies.

There is, therefore, a rich variety of models, theories, techniques and concepts available for use by the practising manager in helping him solve business problems. He will need to appreciate the strengths and weaknesses of all these ideas which jostle for his attention. The choice of approach is clearly a matter of judgment and the application of these diverse ideas to complex business problems requires skills that can only come through experience.

According to Jerome Bruner (1972), the most urgent task of education is the development of what he calls 'disciplined intuition'. Bruner foresees that in the modern world computers will run off routine tasks of analysis, leaving the more difficult, ill-defined, non-programmable problems to be solved. When dealing with these problems, men will be served best by 'a vigorous and courageous intuitive gift, refined through practice' (page 113). The wider the range of techniques and ideas at his command, the greater will be the manager's scope for creative thinking, but he should always be prepared to explore entirely new directions of thought. No theory drawn from past experience may be taken as being literally applicable to a current problem. Training in the creative use of concepts is as important as the acquisition of a basic stock of 'relevant' ideas and techniques. In a time of rapid technological and social change the manager must be able to apply his knowledge and skills in situations where the future is uncertain and the past may be irrelevant.

Small Print's Main Products

Phototypesetters

Phototypesetting is a method of composing material for printing which involves the use of a computer bank of film images of the characters used in printing. By photography, the images are transferred to a film which is then used as the printing master. Phototypesetting may be compared with the traditional 'hot metal' method of printing where the linotype machine moulds the letters on to metal which forms a solid slug representing one line of printed material.

Phototypesetting Peripherals

A number of peripheral units may be linked with the typesetter. These include: input keyboards, line printers, disc storage units, on-line keyboards, paper punches, magnetic tape units and visual display units (VDU's).

Software

Computer programmes are available covering such typographical functions as tabulation, indentation, justification and hyphenation. The hardware (phototypesetters and peripherals) and its associated software, together form a complete photo-composition system.

The Stages of Photocomposition

1. The material to be printed is typed out on a keyboard. This input may go direct into a visual display unit, be reproduced on a paper tape or lead to the production of a magnetic tape.

2. The input may be edited on a VDU (rather like a television screen) to correct page layout, rearrange columns, allow space for photographs, etc.

3. The user selects the appropriate typeface and its size:

e.g. 'Times Roman 8 point'

ABCDEFGHIJKLM
NOPQRSTUVWXYZ
abcdefghijklm
nopqrstuvwxyz

The library of character images is sorted by the computer and each required character, enlarged to the appropriate type size, is photographed.

4. The process of phototypesetting has produced a printing master on film or photographic paper. The master is usually printed by the web-offset method.

Colour Scanners

A colour photograph or transparency is scanned by the machine and separate plates for each colour are produced. Colour scanners can be pre-programmed to allow for the varying characteristics of paper, ink and press.

APPENDIX 2

The Small Print
Case Study

The main reason for the introduction of material about 'Small Print' during the course of the book has been to illustrate relationships between the various functions of a modern manufacturing business rather than to present a business problem for discussion. However, now that the presentation is complete, the reader may wish to review all this material and make positive suggestions about the company's objectives, strategy, organisation and operation.

Imagine that you have been appointed as a management consultant by the board of Small Print Ltd with the following terms of reference:

1. To investigate the cause of the deterioration in the company's financial position.
2. To formulate a revised set of long-term objectives for the company.
3. To review the company's organisational structure.
4. To make any recommendations for increasing the effectiveness of the current operation of the business with particular reference to the marketing, production, personnel and finance functions, so that the company will be able to achieve its long-term objectives.

The following *programme of investigation* is suggested:

(i)   Review chapters 2 − 4 to obtain a general impression of the business, its development, products, markets, organisation, current objectives and strategy.

(ii)   Re-read carefully Chapter 8 paying particular attention to trends in the company's balance sheets and income statements. The ratios which have been calculated from this information will suggest matters for further investigation, e.g. the decline in gross profit margins might suggest that pricing policies and production costs should be examined. List all these possible explanations for the worsening financial performance of the company.

(iii)   Investigate as many of these possibilities as you can from the information available in Chapters 5, 6, 7 and 8. Under 'marketing', for instance, it will be necessary to consider all the elements in the 'marketing mix' in turn. Are there any *disadvantages* in having such a high proportion of export sales? There may not be sufficient detail for a full analysis of all matters might be relevant, but in some cases it will be possible to make reasonable assumptions from hints given in the text. Otherwise it will only be possible to note matters which require further investigation.

(iv)   You should now be in a position to list the *most likely* causes of the company's declining financial performance.

(v)   Re-read Chapter 4 and consult some of the references to corporate planning and business strategy (e.g. Ansoff 1965). What is the 'distinctive competence' of Small Print and what are the main features of its business environment? Should the company alter its basic strategy given its present financial difficulties? Suggest a revised set of objectives remembering that these should relate to the long-term development of the company. It may be possible to solve the immediate financial problem by declaring all the research and development staff redundant, but this would hardly be a satisfactory long-term objective for a company engaged in advanced technology. It will be impossible to formulate a full 'hierarchy' of objectives in precise terms but make sure that your suggestions are internally consistent.

(vi)   Detailed information about the current organisation of the company is limited. The organisation chart (figure 4.1), the list of employees (table 2.1) and the comments on the organisation of the production and marketing functions in Chapter 5 are the main sources. Your recommendations for restructuring the organisation must therefore be somewhat tentative; state clearly any assumptions you make. Note the general comments on organisation structure (Chapter 4) and the problem of size (Chapter 7). One of the recommended texts on business organisation (e.g. O'Shaughnessy 1976) should be consulted for a fuller analysis of the problems of organisational design.

(vii)   The final task is to examine the separate business functions and make any recommendations which will improve their effectiveness. Within each of the main functions (marketing, production, finance and personnel) it is possible to identify more specialised functions: export marketing, production control, quality control, purchasing, equipment servicing, credit control, industrial relations and many others. Make specific recommendations about the organisation and operation of some of these functions consulting the specialist texts in the reading list where appropriate. What management techniques might be introduced to improve the efficiency of a particular activity? Make sure that any suggestions you make are consistent with the long-term objectives which you have set for the company. You will not have sufficient information to translate all your recommendations into operating budgets for 1976. It will, however, be useful to refer back to figure 8.2 in order to check the main inter-relationships between the various functions for the business. Is it now possible to revise some of the budget targets contained in figure 8.2 in the light of your detailed recommendations about Small Print's strategy, objectives and operations?

Case Study References

The following index gives page references to all aspects of the Small Print case study:

Suggestions
for Further Reading

1. Business and Systems Theory

The collection of readings by Beishon (1976) is the most convenient general introduction to the study of systems behaviour. Kast and Rosenzweig (1974) is a business organisation textbook which adopts a systems approach to the subject.

The idea of the socio-technical system is best introduced through Trist and Bamford's (1951) classic description of working methods in the coal industry. Emery and Trist (1960) give a more general statement of the principle.

Many of the readings in the Beishon (1976) and Emery (1969) collections discuss the idea of open systems. Emery and Trist (1965) suggest a conceptual framework for analysing organisational environments. It is an important article containing two valuable case histories, despite its forbidding title. The subject of relations between the enterprise and other organisations in the environment may be studied further in the Evan (1976) collection of readings.

2. Business Organisation

O'Shaughnessy (1976) describes and compares the classical, human relations, systems and contingency approaches to business organisation. Pugh (1971) is a valuable selection of original sources on the subject, and Pugh (1964) summarises in a concise form the ideas of the major writers on organisations. Katz and Kahn (1966) is a classic survey of the contribution of social psychology to organisation theory.

Child (1977) analyses practical organisational problems drawing on the findings of recent research in business and government organisations.

3.   Business Strategy

Ansoff's (1965) text must now rank as a classic on the subject; it may be supplemented by the same writer's collection of readings (Ansoff 1969). Argenti (1968) is a useful, practical introduction to corporate planning.

4.   Business and Society

Child (1969) provides a concise review of the extensive literature on the theme of 'The Business Enterprise in Modern Industrial Society'. The collections of readings on 'Industrial Man' by Burns (1969) and on 'The Modern Business Enterprise' by Gilbert (1972) offer a convenient means of access to some of this literature.

The reader who is interested in future developments should refer to the following important works:

> *The New Industrial State,*   Galbraith (1967)
> *The Coming of Post-Industrial Society,*   Bell (1973)
> *Social Limits to Growth,*   Hirsch (1977)

In each case the title of the book is a succinct statement of an important strand in the debate.

5.   Economics and Marketing

Samuelson (1976), McCormick et al. (1974), Robinson and Eatwell (1973), and Lipsey (1975) are amongst the best known first year undergraduate economics textbooks. Farquhar (1975) is a short introduction to the theory and practice of economic management, with particular reference to UK economic policy since the war. Prest and Coppock (1976) is a survey of the major UK economic institutions and Allen (1970) provides a useful introduction to the study of British industrial structure. Curwen (1974) is a convenient introduction to managerial economics.

Kotler (1976) is a comprehensive study of the marketing function. Simmonds and Leighton (1973) is an interesting collection of marketing case studies. Tookey (1975) deals specifically with marketing for export and Wilson (1965) with the marketing of industrial products.

6.   Production and Operations Management

Johnson *et al.* (1974) introduce the subject of production and operations management within a general systems framework. Lockyer (1974) and Wild (1971) deal more fully with the practice of production management including the most important production management techniques (work study, network analysis, etc.). Finch (1976) is a useful 'encyclopaedia' of general management techniques.

There are innumerable books on the techniques of operational research. Littlechild (1977) is a valuable introduction to the subject for the reader with a limited mathematical background. It stresses the managerial application of operational research and contains a number of case histories. Loomba (1976) is a clear guide to linear programming techniques.

7.   Personnel and Industrial Relations

French (1974) and Thomason (1975) are general textbooks covering the principles and practice of personnel management. Stainer (1971) deals more specifically with manpower planning. Fox (1974) is highly critical of much current personnel management practice.

Lupton (1971) assesses the contribution of the social sciences to management practice, and Vroom and Deci (1970) contains selections from some of the main contributors to the debate about motivation to work. Argyle (1972) draws together in a convenient introductory text the main research findings in the general field of the social psychology of work. McCarthy (1969) is a useful short introduction to the system of industrial relations in Britain. Clegg (1972) is a more comprehensive text covering the same ground. The collection of readings edited by Barrett *et al.* (1975) places the subject of industrial relations in its social context.

8. Finance

Bull (1976) is a general introduction to accounting principles and practice for the business student. Langley (1973) is a more elementary, Hindmarch *et al.* (1977) a more advanced, and Glautier and Underdown (1976) a more extensive, treatment of this material.

Sizer (1969) is recommended as a convenient introduction to management accounting, Carsberg (1975) to the use of accounting information in decision making, and Hopwood (1974) to the behavioural aspects of accounting.

The above selection is confined to books published in the UK. Amongst the numerous American texts adopting a 'managerial' approach to accounting, Horngren (1974) and Bierman and Drebin (1972) can be recommended.

9. Government and Law

A number of books provide a general description of the political system in the UK. Mackintosh (1974) relates the development of the constitution to contemporary political events, whereas Rose (1974) adopts a more functional approach to the subject. Thomas (1976) includes an analysis of the current relationship between government and industry. Milliband (1969) gives a more 'radical' account of the role of the state in capitalist society.

Smith and Keenan (1975) and James (1976) give a general introduction to the principles of English law. More specialised topics of interest to the student of business are: commercial law — Borrie (1975); employment law — Hepple and O'Higgins (1976); company law — Gower (1969) and the law relating to industrial injuries — Munkman (1975).

Friedmann (1972) is an ambitious attempt to analyse the interaction between legal development and social change. The section concerned with 'economic power, the state and the law' is of particular interest to the student of business.

References

Accounting Standards Steering Committee (1975), *The Corporate Report*, Institute of Chartered Accountants in England and Wales.

Aguilar F.J. (1967), *Scanning the Business Environment*, Collier Macmillan.

Allen G.C. (1970), *The Structure of Industry in Britain*, Longmans (3rd edn).

Ansoff H.I. (1965), *Corporate Strategy*, McGraw-Hill (Penguin 1968).

Ansoff H.I. (ed.) (1969), *Business Strategy*, Penguin.

Argenti J. (1968), *Corporate Planning*, Allen and Unwin.

Argyle M. (1972), *The Social Psychology of Work*, Penguin.

Argyris (1952), *The Impact of Budgets on People*, The School of Business & Public Administration, Cornell University.

Barrett B. *et al.* (ed.) (1975), *Industrial Relations and the Wider Society*, Collier Macmillan.

Beishon J. and Peters G. (eds) (1976), *Systems Behaviour*, Harper and Row (2nd edn).

Bell D. (1973), *The Coming of Post-Industrial Society*, Basic Books 1973 (Penguin 1976).

Bierman H. and Drebin A.R. (1972), *Managerial Accounting*, Collier Macmillan (2nd edn).

Blauner R. (1964), *Alienation and Freedom: The Factory Worker and His Industry*, University of Chicago Press.

de Bono E. (1972), *PO: Beyond Yes and No.* Simon and Schuster (Penguin 1973).

Borrie G.J. (1975), *Commercial Law*, Butterworths (4th edn).

Bruner J. (1972), *Relevance of Education*, Allen and Unwin (Penguin 1974).

Bull R.J. (1976), *Accounting in Business*, Butterworths (3rd edn).

Bullock, Lord (Chairman) (1977), *Report of the Committee of Inquiry on Industrial Democracy*, HMSO.

Burnham J. (1941), *The Managerial Revolution*, Putnam.

Burns T. (ed.) (1969), *Industrial Man*, Penguin.

Burns T. and Stalker G.M. (1961), *The Management of Innovation*, Tavistock.

Burns T. (1966), 'On the plurality of social systems' in Lawrence J.R. (ed.), *Operational Research and the Social Sciences*, Tavistock (included in Gilbert 1972).

Carsberg B. (1975), *Economics of Business Decisions*, Penguin.

Child J. (1969), *The Business Enterprise in Modern Industrial Society*, Collier Macmillan.

Child J. (1977), *Organisation: A Guide to Problems and Practice*, Harper and Row.

Clegg H.A. (1976), *The System of Industrial Relations in Great Britain*, Basil Blackwell (3rd edn).

Curwen P.J. (1974), *Managerial Economics*, Macmillan.

Cyert R.M. and March J.G. (1963), *A Behavioural Theory of the Firm*, Prentice-Hall.

Denning B.W. (1968), 'The integration of business studies at the conceptual level', *Journal of Management Studies*, Feb., Vol. 5, No. 1.

Emery F.E. (ed.) (1969), *Systems Thinking*, Penguin.

Emery F.E. and Trist E.L. (1960), 'Socio-technical systems' in Churchman C.W. and Verhulst M. (eds), *Management Science, Models and Techniques*, Vol. 2, Pergamon (included in Emery 1969).

Emery F.E. and Trist E.L. (1965), 'The casual texture of organisational environments', *Human Relations*, Vol. 18, pp 21 − 32 (included in Emery 1969).

Evan W.M. (ed.) (1976), *Inter-organisational Relations*, Penguin.

Farquhar J.D. (1975), *The National Economy*, Philip Allan.

Finch F. (1976), *A Concise Encyclopaedia of Management Techniques*, Heinemann.

Fox A. (1966), 'Industrial sociology and industrial relations', Research Paper 3, *Royal Commission on Trade Unions and Employers' Associations*, HMSO.

Fox A. (1974), *Man Mismanagement*, Hutchinson.

French W. (1974), *The Personnel Management Process*, Houghton Mifflin (3rd edn).

Friedman M. (1963), *Capitalism and Freedom*, University of Chicago Press.

Friedmann W. (1972), *Law in a Changing Society*, Stevens and Penguin (2nd edn).

Galbraith J.K. (1967), *The New Industrial State*, Hamish Hamilton (Penguin 1969).

Gellerman S.W. (1974), *Behavioural Science in Management*, Penguin.

Gilbert M. (ed.) (1972), *The Modern Business Enterprise*, Penguin.

Glautier M.W.E. and Underdown B. (1976), *Accounting Theory and Practice*, Pitman.

Gower L.C.B. (1969), *The Principles of Modern Company Law*, Stevens (3rd edn).

Grant W.P. and Marsh D. (1975), 'The politics of the CBI: 1974 and after', *Government and Opposition*, Vol. 10, No. 1, Winter.

Grove J.W. (1962), *Government and Industry in Britain*, Longmans.

Hayek F.A. (1960), 'The corporation in democratic society' in Ashen M. and Bach G. (eds), *Management and Corporations 1985*, McGraw-Hill.

Hepple B.A. and O'Higgins P. (1976), *Employment Law*, Sweet and Maxwell (2nd edn).

Herzberg F. (1966), *Work and The Nature of Man*, World Publishing Co.

Hindmarch A., Atchison M. and Marke R. (1977), *Accounting – An Introduction*, Macmillan.

Hirsch F. (1977), *Social Limits to Growth*, Routledge and Kegan Paul.

Hirst P.H. (1965), in Archambault R.D. (ed.) *Philosophical Analysis and Education*, Routledge and Kegan Paul.

Hopwood A. (1974), *Accounting and Human Behaviour*, Accountancy Age.

Horngren C.T. (1974), *Accounting for Managerial Control*, Prentice-Hall (3rd edn).

James P.S. (1976), *Introduction to English Law*, Butterworths (9th edn).

Jay A. (1967), *Management and Machiavelli*, Hodder and Stoughton.

Johnson R.A., Newell W.T. and Vergin R.C. (1974), *Production and Operations Management: A Systems Concept*, Houghton Mifflin.

Kast F.E. and Rosenzweig J.E. (1974), *Organisation and Management: A Systems Approach*, McGraw-Hill (2nd edn).

Katz D. and Kahn R.L. (1966), *The Social Psychology of Organisations*, Wiley.

Kotler P. (1976), *Marketing Management: Analysis, Planning and Control*, Prentice-Hall (3rd edn).

Langley F.P. (1973), *Introduction to Accounting for Business Studies*, Butterworths (2nd edn).

Levitt T. (1960), 'Marketing Myopia' in *Harvard Business Review*, Aug.

Likert R. (1961), *New Patterns of Management*, McGraw-Hill.

Lipsey R.G. (1975), *An Introduction to Positive Economics*, Weidenfeld and Nicolson (4th edn).

Littlechild S.C. (ed.) (1977), *Operational Research for Managers*, Philip Allan.

Lockyer K.G. (1974), *Factory and Production Management*, Pitman.

Loomba N.P. (1976), *Linear Programming: A Managerial Perspective*, Macmillan (2nd edn).

Lupton T. (1971), *Management and the Social Sciences*, Penguin (2nd edn).

McCarthy (ed.) (1969), *Industrial Relations in Britain*, Lyon Grant and Green.

McGregor D. (1960), *The Human Side of Enterprise*, McGraw-Hill.

McCormick B. *et al.* (1974), *Introducing Economics*, Penguin.

McClelland D.C. (1961), *The Achieving Society*, Van Nostrand.

Mackenzie W.J.M. (1967), *Politics and Social Science*, Penguin.

Mackintosh J.P. (1974), *The Government and Politics of Britain*, Hutchinson (3rd edn).

Maslow A.H. (1954), *Motivation and Personality*, Harper.

Mayo E. (1949), *The Social Problems of an Industrial Civilization*, Routledge and Kegan Paul.

Milliband D.R. (1969), *The State in Capitalist Society*, Weidenfeld and Nicolson.

Mishan E.J. (1967), *The Cost of Economic Growth*, Staples Press (Penguin 1969).

Munkman J.(1975), *Employers' Liability at Common Law*. Butterworths (8th edn).

Pollard S. (1965), *The Genesis of Modern Management*, Edward Arnold (Penguin 1968).

Prest A.R. and Coppock D.J. (eds) (1976), *The UK Economy: A Manual of Applied Economics*, Weidenfeld and Nicolson (6th edn).

Pugh D.S. (ed.) (1971), *Organisation Theory*, Penguin.

Pugh D.S. *et al.* (1964), *Writers on Organisations*, Hutchinson (Penguin 1971).

Robinson J. and Eatwell J. (1973), *An Introduction to Modern Economics*, McGraw-Hill.

Rose R. (1974), *Politics in England Today*, Faber.

Samuelson P.A. (1976), *Economics*, McGraw-Hill (10th edn).

O'Shaughnessy J. (1976), *Patterns of Business Organisation*, Allen and Unwin.

Schon D.A. (1971), *Beyond the Stable State*, Temple Smith.

Simmonds K. and Leighton D. (1973), *Case Problems in Marketing*, Nelson.

Sizer J. (1969), *An Insight into Management Accounting*, Penguin

Smith K. and Keenan D.J. (1975), *English Law*, Pitman (5th edn).

Stainer G. (1971), *Manpower Planning: The Management of Human Resources*, Heinemann.

Taylor F.W. (1947), *Scientific Management*, Harper and Row.

Thomas R.E. (1976), *The Government of Business*, Philip Allan.

Thomason G. (1975), *A Textbook of Personnel Management*, Institute of Personnel Management.

Tookey D. (1975), *Export Marketing Decisions*, Penguin.

Trist E.L. and Bamforth K.W. (1951), 'Some social and psychological consequences of the longwall method of coal getting', *Human Relations*, Vol. 4 pp 3–38, quoted in Burns T. (ed.) (1969).

Vroom V.H. and Deci E.L. (eds) (1970), *Management and Motivation*, Penguin

Wild R. (1971), *The Techniques of Production Management*, Holt, Rinehart and Winston.

Wilson A. (ed.) (1965), *The Marketing of Industrial Products*, Hutchinson.

Index